The *Western* Legends Live On

Tales & Interviews with the Cowboy Stars of the Silver Screen

20 YEAR EDITION
UPDATED & REVISED
2017

Charlie LeSueur

Copyright © 1999 by Charlie LeSueur

First Printing 1999

Lazy Susan Productions

Revised 2017

Second Printing 2017

All rights reserved. No part of this book may be reproduced in any form without written permission from the author or his agents, except for brief quotations used in newspapers or magazines in connection with a review.

Published by Norseman Publications

Original ISBN 1-885162-25-1

Current ISBN-13: 978-1544869537

Printed in the United States of America

This book I lovingly dedicate to my Dad, who instilled a love for westerns in me, to my wife, Dawn, who has allowed me to keep it, to Johnny & Jo Western for inspiration and Buck & Goldie Taylor from whom the inspiration for the title of this book was taken.

TABLE OF CONTENTS

FORWARD
by Johnny Western

===============

INTRODUCTION

===============

Chapter One
Regrets & Missed Opportunities

===============

Chapter Two
REX ALLEN
Battle Hymn of Republic Pictures
Walt Disney-Lands Rex &
"Where's Snuff?"

===============

Chapter Three
HARRY CAREY, JR.
Reminiscing about Harry Sr., John Wayne, John Ford, Ben Johnson & the Career of a Supporting Player

Chapter Four
LASH LaRUE
Did your Mother Ever Meet Humphrey Bogart?
Don Barry Sees 'Red,'
& "Fuzzy was Fuzzy!"

===================

Chapter Five
ROY ROGERS
A Tale of a Tail,
& the Wrong Cowboy

===================

Chapter Six
JOHN SMITH
The Name's Sherman... Slim Sherman
From Dancer to Actor to Icon, Robert Fuller
The Rita Hayworth Incident
Hell, Hath No Fury Like Hathaway!

===================

Chapter Seven
BUCK TAYLOR
The Legends Live On
From Cannonball to Newly
Chauffeur to Water Colors

Chapter Eight
JOHNNY WESTERN
From "Grand Old 'Autry'" to "Will Play for 'Cash'" to "A Real 'Boone' to Johnny's Career"

======

EPILOGUE

FOREWARD

Johnny Western

I have always said the song; "My Heroes Have Always Been Cowboys" could have and should have been written for me. At least the Saturday afternoon and TV cowboys part of it should have. I was born in 1934, so I was just right for the age group that really loved those Saturday matinees at the West Theater in my hometown of Northfield, Minnesota. Jesse James and the Younger Brothers tried to take the bank there in 1876 and got shot to pieces and I guess I grew up with that legend. So, when I could gather up the price for a movie and popcorn, it was off to the theater for this young boy and I lived and loved every minute of it. I couldn't have imagined at that time that by the time I was thirteen and fourteen years old, I would actually meet and work with the stars of those films that so enchanted my mind. But I did! And I have the greatest memories in the world of those times.

I met Roy Rogers and Dale Evans when I was fourteen; Gene Autry when I was fifteen, and Rex Allen when I was sixteen. They were all on my radio show at KDHL in South Minnesota in those days, and they all said that if I ever came to Hollywood to look them up and they would try to help me get started out there. Tex Ritter came by when I was seventeen and took me on some show dates with him on the Drive-In Theater circuit and that was it. I had to go and I did when I was nineteen. I packed up bag and baggage, left my radio and TV shows behind to take a chance on tinsel town. And those guys did help me; all of 'em. I felt my first earthquake while visiting at Tex Ritter's house in the valley. Rex Allen and I did shows together and Roy Rogers and The Sons of the Pioneers and I were singing together at a private party when Gene Autry heard me and put me under contract when Johnny Bond retired in '56. The day that Dick Jones called and said that Gene wanted to see me at his office is as vivid to me today as it was in June of '56 when he called. My road tours with Gene, Gail "Annie Oakley" Davis, The Cass Co. Boys and Carl Cotner were the greatest thing that ever happened to me. When Gene retired, he put me with his agent for movie and TV work and made the rest of my life happen. Yes, Virginia, childhood dreams can come true! And they did; all of them.

Right at that same time, I was spending a lot of time with Audie Murphy, who gave me my first

Colt 45 six-gun, which I treasure to this day. I was spending more time with Ben Johnson at his place, and that meant I got to spend some time with Harry Carey, Jr. and his wife, Marilyn. New Year's Eve at their place was something else. What a thrill to be there with those folks who remain dear friends today. We've lost Uncle Ben and Aunt Carol, but the memories will never die.

TV took over from the Saturday heroes and I got into the saddle with more good friends like Dale Robertson, Jim Arness, Dennis Weaver and, of course, Richard Boone. Did you ever imagine what it would be like to play cowboy on film with those guys and actually get paid for it? Maynard, it does not get any better than that!

It wasn't all sweetness and light however. Recently, Robert Fuller and I were at a Film Festival together in Charlotte, North Carolina and we got on-the-subject-of what happened to his co-star, John Smith. Charlie, will outline that story for you in the following pages. Lash LaRue was one of our great cowboy heroes whose fate could have been different had he not looked so much like Bogart. He once asked me for an autographed picture to put on the wall of his motel in Reno when I was appearing there for a few days and staying at LaRue's lodge. I couldn't believe that anyone like Lash would ever ask me for an autograph. He had been out of show biz for years and things had changed for him, but not in my eyes.

I met Buck Taylor and his *Gunsmoke* gang in Cheyenne one year when I was performing at 'Frontier Days.' The next time I saw him was in Flagstaff, Arizona at the Little America Hotel, and his Dad, the Great 'Dub' Taylor was with him. Years had passed, but it was like the day before yesterday once we started talking.

This of course was the period-of-time when America still held some values and the good guys in the white (or black) hats! Today, it's all changed. We have-to collect old TV video tapes and records at festivals in order to hold on to those wonderful days that the kids of this era will never know. I live in Wichita, Kansas and we have the best looking female district attorney in America. Her name is Nola Foulston and she called me one day asking me to make her a tape of the best real cowboy songs ever recorded by the original singers, including, Autry, Allen, Rogers, Ritter, etc. She said, "I don't want my son, Andrew, growing up thinking Luke Skywalker is the Great American Hero. I want him to know who the great cowboy stars were, like I did when I was growing up." I wish there were several million more just like her. My wife, Jo, has-to constantly move things out of our video cabinets to make room for more stuff that I pick up at every festival I perform at around America.

When you are reading my friend Charlie LeSueur's book, I hope you will look back fondly on those great days when our cowboy heroes were everything to us. They formed our thoughts, our lives, and our dreams with their screen images. The horses, with the silver saddles, the colorful clothes, the guns and gun belts, the guitars and songs, and that certain look they all gave you from the screen that said to you, "Everything is going to be all right." We may never be able to totally recreate those days again on TV or the Big Screen, but those of us who are still out there doing shows and festivals and the like, and still making records, are going to give it the old college try! I was the luckiest guy in the world to get paid for doing what I probably would have done for free had it not worked out that way. As my friend, Ranger Doug of 'Riders in the Sky' fame always says, "It's the Cowboy Way!"

Johnny Western
Great Empire Broadcasting Inc.
Wichita, Kansas, America

INTRODUCTION

As I re-read the kind words, Johnny Western, wrote for my fore-ward, he is enjoying a well-deserved retirement not far from where I am living here in the Valley of the Sun. As-a-matter of fact much has changed since I first wrote this book and I am going to endeavor to bring you all up-to-date.

Some of it is quite surprising in concept. Back in 1998 when I wrote the first edition of "Legends" I was a relatively young man who had been living a simple dream of interviewing so many of my childhood idols; little did I dream I would become friends with many of them. One of those idols I wrote some unkind things about in the first edition, which I plan on rectifying here-in.

Still, for purposes of integrity, I am going to leave some things as they are – with a bit of a "catch-up" at the end of the chapter.

While this book is filled with interviews, I think you'll be surprised at how much other information it has on all aspects of the silver screen cowboys many of us grew up watching on TV, and some even at the neighborhood movie theater.

While many of the people I talk about are no longer with us, the title of this tome is more appropriate than ever, for the "legends truly do live on." I hope you enjoy the tales...

I've been blessed with being able to spend time with some of my childhood favorites like, Ben Johnson, Harry Carey, Jr., Roy Rogers, Gene Autry, Rex Allen, Denver Pyle, John Smith, and Lash LaRue, just to name a few. As I look at this list of names, people that I write about in this book, I realize that we're losing a lot of our heroes.

That's why I believe western festivals, such as The National Festival of the West, serve an extremely important function, not to mention the wholesome fun that can be found there. As a so called, "Baby Boomer," my generation was the last to enjoy many of these stars in action, but the legacy that has been left can still be enjoyed by all ages.

We can forever enjoy Roy and Gene singing a tune and saving the day, or Ben Johnson mumbling something under his breath as John Wayne barks out an order to him. Denver Pyle will always be there for us to hiss, or laugh at, depending on what character he's playing. John Smith will forever be the handsome hero, no matter what tragedy struck his later life. And Lash... will always be... Lash, for better or worse.

This book is not the last word on any of these people...far from it. What I have endeavored to do is relate my experiences with these stars and, in some cases, explore their background, make comments on my feelings about them, and use other friends and celebrities' comments and memories as well.

I started out helping with the advertising for The Festival of the West and ended up using whatever movie knowledge I have, to help with the celebrity question and answer sessions; a big part of the festival each year. It's been fun and interesting to get the reactions from the stars when I ask them something they didn't figured anybody would know...like Denver Pyle who ended up calling me his "personal encyclopedia."

The comments the stars make are interesting and informative. Many times, the things they say are very personal therefore they should be recorded for those of us fans who would like to learn all we can about the heroes of our childhood before these people can no longer share them.

Hopefully, with a little help from my friends...the stars themselves...I'll be able to provide some interesting tidbits you may not have known before. For example: what 1940's western film star was featured in a porno film, or what other popular actor claims to have originally been scheduled to play Marshal Dillon in *Gunsmoke* (no, not John Wayne). What actor was the second most decorated soldier in World War Two, following Audie Murphy? What up and coming actor's career was ruined by an insensitive director? These are the types of things that I have included in this book.

I'd like to thank those that made this book possible. I'm sure I'll forget some, so please forgive me. I'd like to start by thanking Johnny Western for giving me the idea for this book. You can read how it came about in his chapter. Next, I'd like to thank Mary Brown, the head honcho for The National Festival of the West, for having faith in me and letting me handle the question and answer sessions at the festival for these many years. Next, there's Hank and Sharyn Sheffer for their help and expertise in putting this book together; they knew I had it in me long before I did. Marshall Terrill, author of the definitive biographies on Steve McQueen, for his support in writing this book. Big thanks to Buck and Goldie Taylor for their encouragement, and the inspiration for the book's title; and, of course, all the stars who allowed me to pick their brain over the past eight years.

The one person I'd like to thank the most is my wife, Dawn, who has stood by me and supported this effort through a lot of procrastination on my part. Well, my love, here…it…is!!

Charlie LeSueur
March 30th, 2017

CHAPTER 1
Regrets & Missed Opportunities

A passion for western movies, the stars, and all the history within that genre were a part of my life long before I embarked on what has turned out to be a dream career. As you read this chapter, keep in mind I had no idea what would lay ahead for me, otherwise I would have spent more time asking questions of the actors I worked with; likewise, if I knew I would still be hard at it twenty years later I would have tempered some of my original remarks in print.

I would like to say I aimed for this life I have, but I didn't...it happened and is still continually evolving. The original sections of this book you are reading are written by a real novice...not that I'm an expert now by any means, but at least I have a better idea what is in my future. I have spruced up some areas that truly make me wince but other than that this chapter, and the book itself, is as it was almost 20 years ago.

"What are you going to do with all-of-this useless trivia?" That's what my mother would ask me; to be fair to her, she would ask that in response to all the time I sat in front of the TV set or at the movie theater instead of doing my homework.

Now, however, here I was in front of an audience and beside a dais of familiar faces that were a big part of all my "useless trivia." The saying "being at the right place at the right time," means a whole lot more to me since becoming a part of The National Festival of the West in Scottsdale, Arizona.

Before that, I had been in a few films and TV shows which featured some pretty heavy hitters as far as films and television goes, Gene Barry, Ed

Ames, Dorothy Malone, David Opatoshu, Brock Peters, Whit Bissell, Peter Mark Richmond, Rick Jason – names that meant something at that time, still do to film fans.

I remember Dorothy Malone would walk around the set of *Sodom and Gomorrah* by Lake Powell bemoaning the fact that she was always getting roles where she had to suffer. This would not be an exception, the wife of Lot (Ed Ames) she of course would end up as a pillar of salt.

Then there was urban veteran character actor, David Opatoshu, who was playing my father. How could I tell him that complaining about your meal being undercooked and sending it back to the kitchen at Lake Powell's Wahweap Lodge probably wasn't a wise decision; I can imagine the "proper care" of his meal taking place in the kitchen before he got it back.

Unfortunately, even though I had the opportunity, I was more interested in an acting career at the time and just didn't make any effort to talk with these stars. As a result, I missed many chances to question esteemed bodies of Hollywood history about their careers and the stars they in turn had worked with.

A case in point: 1977, one of my great missed opportunities happened when I did a film called, *The Hi-Riders*. The movie was a real bomb and the director was a hack and a terrible person. Also, due to the inexperience of the stunt coordinator, he died doing the very last stunt on the picture, two weeks before he was to be married. The film is dedicated to him. Big deal!

Never the less, the film is filled with former stars: Mel Ferrer, Stephen McNally, Ralph Meeker and Neville Brand; I'm told Victor Mature had a role, but backed out. It was a wise decision. This was at a time before pre-recorded modes of video became the norm and these stars were used in low-budget films that would appeal to 2nd feature billing and European release where these American stars were still big names and would look good on marquees.

As I said, the director was a no talent and the nastiest person you'd ever meet. I won't mention his name, but it still shows up from time to time on low budget grade Z flicks. In case you can't tell, I didn't like him.

I was an acting student at the time in Los Angeles and my acting teacher was part of the film crew so his students, me included, were given an opportunity to be a part of the "cast."

The Hi-Riders is about a car gang who take over a town and terrorizes it. It's a variation on the old motorcycle gang films of the 1960's.

The students were given parts of one of the titled gang; even so, we were little more than extras. When we weren't working in a scene, the assistant (emphasis on the first three letters) director would make sure we were kept busy shining up the cars, so they would look pretty; it was our job in exchange for being granted the opportunity to be in this epic. In return, we were awarded box lunches with stale sandwiches, while the main actors were given hot meals.

The one thing that I enjoyed about the film was working around the featured actors. Here was Stephen (Horace) McNally, who had acted with the likes of Jimmy Stewart in *Winchester '73* (1950), Audie Murphy in *The Duel at Silver Creek* (1952) and *Hell Bent for Leather* (1960), and James Cagney in *Tribute to a Badman* (1956), and Ralph

Meeker who appeared with Jimmy Stewart in the classic Anthony Mann western *The Naked Spur* (1957).

At the time of *The Hi-Riders* it was obvious that Meeker was ill. At first, I thought he was showing up to the set drunk. On the first day, he showed up he was stiff and unsteady when he walked; he was barely able to move his head from left to right; he held one arm in a bent claw like position and he shuffled slowly and carefully on very unsure legs. He walked past me smiled and said, *"Hi."* Later that day, I realized that he was cold stone sober and suffering from some illness. It appeared to me that he probably had a progressive form of arthritis. I thought this for many years until recently when I read that his condition was due to a serious stroke.

Ralph Meeker in "The Naked Spur"

Nevertheless, when the director called "Action!" he had full motion. It must have been painful for him, but he never showed it. The moment the director yelled "Cut!", his fluid movement ceased and he would literally shuffle off. If you look carefully at his later film appearances you can tell he had problems, but you really have to look for it.

On August 5th, 1988, he died from a heart attack. Ralph Meeker played the bad guy quite a bit, but like many others who appeared as the heavy, like Jan Merlin and Myron Healey, off screen he was a very nice gentleman.

Neville Brand

Stephen McNally and Mel Ferrer kept to themselves, but Neville Brand, although quiet, seemed to like to stay on set with the crew. My only remembrance of him is when he was sitting outside the San Fernando Valley bar where we were shooting; he played the bartender which considering his problem with drinking was a funny situation. He was smoking and the assistant director gave orders that nobody but Mr. Brand could smoke on set. Brand seemed to get a chuckle out of that as he flicked his ashes. He had probably had his share of confrontations with A.D.'s before.

The classic Neville Brand story, as told to me by *Laredo* co-star Peter Brown, and related in Harry Carey, Jr.'s excellent book, *Company of Heroes: My Life as an Actor in the John Ford Stock Company*, is about the time when Universal Studios, where Laredo was shot, began the tram tours. This was way before the studio became known more as an amusement park than a studio; the tram tour was all there was at the time.

If there was any filming going on orders where that it had to cease until the tram would pass by. It's hard to believe that the tram took precedence over a film schedule where budgets and time frames are so important. It angered Neville so much that he took it upon himself to go to the "Black Tower" where the studio offices were located and complain. "He wanted them to divert the trams in another direction, but he was told the tours were keeping the studio a float at the time," Peter Brown told me.

The tours continued to pass by the location shooting and the mobile dressing rooms of the stars so Neville decided to take matters into his own hands...literally.

As the tram passed the actor's dressing room one day, he stepped out. Excited to spy a star, the tram announcer made the most of it. "Ladies and gentlemen, there's *Laredo*'s Neville Brand!" Without missing a beat, he unzipped his pants and began urinating in full display as the tram passed by. The next day the tram began taking a brand-new route. Imagine the pictures that might be out there from some fast acting tram tourist.

To be fair, this is the way Harry Carey, Jr. told it on a panel with Johnny Western:

Johnny: *"Crazy Neville, he'd get high if he walked under a Falstaff sign."*

Harry: *"I was on the first Universal Studios tour in 1962, but when it got bigger and bigger, they would drive by movie stars' dressing rooms and Neville was working on Laredo, with Phil Carey. As they drove past Neville's dressing room, he ran out with his gun belt on and nothing else!"*

Could this have been two different incidents? Who knows, but as reporter Maxwell Scott so aptly put it in *The Man Who Shot Liberty Valance*: *"When the Legend becomes fact, print the legend."*

It's become common knowledge now that Neville Brand is credited as being the second most decorated soldier in World War Two right after Audie Murphy. His big break came when he played Al Capone in *The Untouchables* TV program, with Robert Stack, but western fans will always remember him as Reese Bennett in 56 episodes of *Laredo*, with Peter Brown, William Smith, Phil Carey and later Robert Wolders

Unfortunately, all the stars of note from *The Hi-Riders* are gone, except for young lead Darby Hinton. It's sad that I will never have the opportunity to interview any of them and hear the remarkable stories they could tell, stories which could probably fill volumes of books on the subject of western films and television.

Sodom and Gomorrah was an episode of NBC's series called *The Greatest Heroes of the Bible*, which was filmed on a standing biblical set erected on the Utah side of Lake Powell; Sunn Classic Pictures, most identified with the *Grizzly Adams* series, was the production company.

Each week the primetime series would present a highly-dramatized story "ripped" right from the pages of the Bible. I was sharing a chartered plane from Phoenix to the airport at Page, Arizona with the actor Peter Mark Richman, another nice guy, who just a few years before had co-starred with James Franciscus and a relatively unknown Bruce Lee in *Longstreet* (1971–'72).

When we got to the Page airport, as they opened the plane's door, Gene Barry who had been waiting for Richman,

David Opatoshu

stepped right into the plane, shook my hand and introduced himself to me. I'll never forget that.

Ed Ames, who played Mingo in *Daniel Boone* with Fess Parker, was also in the show. He was nice, but aloof. Rick Jason, a rather large actor who had played the second lead in *Combat* with Vic Morrow, had the dubious honor of shoving me off my horse and onto the ground (or rather are doubles did the honors) and then besting me in a brief tussle. He had insisted on driving to the Utah location from Hollywood and always seemed to be "interviewing" young women to be his assistant on set.

As I said before, David Opatoshu, who had appeared in classic films like, *The Brothers Karamazov* (1958), *Exodus* (1960), and *Torn Curtain* (1966), as well as dozens of classic television shows, played my father and would stay on set while I would deliver my lines so I would have someone to relate to on camera. He was wonderful, very open; as was Julie Parrish who I had always had a tremendous crush on and had the room next to mine.

Then there was Dorothy Malone who continued to suffer through her role wondering why she was always given such roles.

I also played a clone in the film *The Lucifer Complex*, which starred Robert Vaughn. He seemed friendly and agreeable, but I was only an extra placed in a long tube with a hose stuck to my navel, (this is how clones received their nourishment in this film). It was a one night shoot for me, for which I never got paid, except in MacDonald's hamburgers.

I was a 27-year-old teenager in a film called *Good-Bye, Franklin High*, in which popular western bad guy Myron Healy had a role as a teacher. Healy is someone I would especially have liked to interview, since he
started out in films with Monte Hale, Charles Starrett, Johnny Mack Brown, Wild Bill Elliott, Roy Barcroft, Andy Clyde, and Smiley Burnette. Imagine the kind of stories he would have! During the fifties, Healy seemed to corner the market on western bad guys along with Lee Van Cleef, Robert J. Wilkie and Jack Elam. I always wondered why he was usually cast as the bad guy when he was such a

good-looking guy, complete with the required square jaw.

Alas, I was in a movie with him and never once thought to approach him to ask about all those stars he had worked with. Healy passed away December 21, 2005.

One last story. In 1974, while staying at the Century Plaza Hotel, the beautiful hotel which stands on what was once part of the 20th Century Fox back-lot, actress Connie Stevens was holding a benefit for her ex-husband James Stacy (*Lancer*). Hollywood had been grooming Stacy for major stardom when a tragic motorcycle accident robbed him of that dream, taking an arm and a leg with it.

The celebrity guest list bridged several generations, and I was star-struck as they all exited the hotel right before my eyes. Gene Kelly, June Allyson, David and Ricky Nelson, Elizabeth Montgomery, Liza Minnelli, Lee Majors and Farrah Fawcett, James Franciscus, Sammy Davis, Jr., Steve McQueen, and John Lennon were there, as was Clint Eastwood, wearing a T-shirt that said, *Thunderbolt and Lightfoot*, to advertise his new film.

It was funny to see Eastwood play to the paparazzi. As they were waiting for the next star(s) to exit one set of doors, a voice came from behind them, "Any stars out here?" The paparazzi turned to see Eastwood, standing at a set of doors at the far end of the hotel. He was poised and ready for action, as the photographers rushed him to grab a picture. These were only a few of the stars there and I was in awe.

The moment I remember the most was when Richard Long (*Bourbon Street Beat, Nanny and the Professor, The Big Valley*) entered the lobby after the event was over, with his wife, actress Mara Corday, and a female friend. A fan walked up to him and asked for his autograph. Long seemed stunned, possibly because even though he turned up on an occasional made for TV movie, he hadn't had a hit television series for a while. The friend must have noticed his astonishment at being asked for an autograph. She turned to Corday and said, *"You see, once a star always a star."* It's true. Richard Long would be a good interview, but he's gone too. December 21, 1974. Myron and Richard seemed to have December 21st in common for leaving us.

The Barkley family of The Big Valley. Top left to right: Lee Majors & Charles Briles. Bottom left to right: Richard Long, Barbara Stanwyck, Peter Breck, & Linda Evans

These were only a few of the stars there and I was in awe. The moment I remember the most was when Richard Long (*Bourbon Street Beat, Nanny and the Professor, The Big Valley*) entered the lobby after the event was over, with his wife, actress Mara Corday, and a female friend. A fan walked up to him and asked for his autograph. Long seemed stunned, possibly because even though he turned up on an occasional made for TV movie, he hadn't had a hit television series for a while. The friend must have noticed his astonishment at being asked for an autograph. She turned to Corday and said, "You see, once a star always a star." It's true.

Richard Long would be a good interview, but he's gone too. December 21, 1974. Myron and Richard seemed to have December 21st in common for leaving us.

I've had a lot of missed opportunities, but I'm making up for it now. I hope I'll be able to interview the stars for years to come. I also hope you enjoy reading this.

You'll find that some of the interviews in this book do not always paint a pretty picture. I try not to hurt, but I do try to be truthful, as in the case of John Smith. I agonized about what to put in his chapter. His life and career were both moving along at a fast pace until what should have been his biggest break began his descent. Mary Brown, bless her heart, relieved me of any worries. She was a very close friend of his and his greatest fan. They shared many talks about John's past. When I approached her about the chapter, she told me that I needed to write the truth. I did, as you will see, but it wasn't easy.

Addendum:

Since this book's first printing I would like to think I have matured and learned to buffer my comments while not trying to revise history. My comments as originally written are in the first publication for those curious. They were unhampered comments of a young aspiring writer who has gotten to know many of these stars on a close basis and realize that there are things to share and things that remain between friends.

Remember as you read what follows that even our heroes were, and are, only human. Despite their mistakes and disappointments, they are "the stuff dreams are made of."

CHAPTER 2
Rex Allen
Battle Hymns of Republic Pictures, Walt Disney-lands Rex & "Where's Snuff?"

I first met Rex Allen sometime in the late 1980's, when I was sent to a Tucson recording studio to produce a television commercial for a local Phoenix, Arizona television program called *The Arizona Cowboy*. Rex would drive in from his ranch in Patagonia and do voice-overs every so often, and so we were scheduled to come down from Phoenix and shoot a quick commercial publicizing something or other, I can't remember what it was.

When Rex arrived at the studio, he hadn't been informed that our commercial was for television and wasn't dressed to do an on-screen endorsement. However, always the pro, he shrugged it off and did the commercial for us anyway.

He was wearing tinted glasses but you could tell that something was wrong with his vision. "I recently fell at home
and damaged my eye." He went on to explain that he has had eye problems since he was a child. "I was so crossed- eyed as a child that when I bawled the tears rolled down by back. They took my left eye right out of the socket to straighten it out." The

recent fall had damaged the eye, a problem that would worsen in the years to come.

Rex and Mary Ellen Kay. Mary Ellen appeared with every "B" Cowboy from the early to mid-1950s. 6 times with Rex.

Despite the eye problem, I handed Rex the script, he looked at it for a minute and delivered the lines perfectly the first time. Not wanting to let him out of my grasp quite that easily, I had him re-do the commercial a few more times with each take done letter perfect.

I knew he was an extremely busy man, but as we were getting ready to leave I just had to ask him one question that I had wondered about for some time.

"Mr. Allen, instead of sidekicks like Gabby Hayes or Smiley Burnette, you had people like Buddy Ebsen, Slim Pickens and 'Alfalfa' Switzer in your films. How did you manage that?"

Rex Allen gave me that famous boyish grin and said just one word, "Money."

The next time I would have a chance to meet Rex Allen, he would explain further how he got people like Buddy Ebsen to be his second banana. I left Tucson that day with a great respect for the Arizona Cowboy.

That next time was at the 1998 National Festival of the West, where Rex Allen was to receive the Cowboy Spirit Award.

In years past, Roy Rogers, Dale Evans, and Gene Autry had each received the Award. Roy couldn't come due to illness and so Dale accepted for them both; Gene graciously accepted his award but was unable to stay and visit with the crowd.

This year, however, we were told that Rex would stay for a Q & A session and sign autographs. As a special bonus my friend Mary Ellen Kay, who had starred in six films with Rex, was to join him.

I had been pushing to get Rex to the Festival of the West for years so when I got the call that both Rex and Ellen would be there I was very excited at the thought of not only visiting with Rex Allen but having Ellen there to reminisce with him about their films.

On the day of the presentation, the meeting between Rex Allen and Mary Ellen Kay was terrific. I was waiting with Ellen when security drove Rex, his wife of five years Virginia, and famed music legend Snuff Garrett to the designated area behind the festival stage.

Snuff Garrett is responsible for the careers of people such as Bobby Vee, Johnny Burnette, and Gary Lewis and the Playboys. He also has scored pictures for Clint Eastwood and television programs like *Evening Shade*; to me he will always be known for his classic song for Roy Rogers, *Hoppy, Gene &*

Me. He recently had scored the film *Hard Time*, which stars Burt Reynolds and Buck Taylor.

Snuff had been a fan of Rex's for a long time and was now a very close associate of his. He was also supposed to serve a different function at the festival that I didn't know about at the time. I'll discuss that function later.

Meanwhile, back at the meeting between Rex and Ellen, without missing a beat he got out of the cart and immediately walked over to her. "Hello, Mary Ellen," he said in that deep rich voice, as he leaned over and gave her a kiss. I almost expected them to break into a duet. I was glad to have been there to see the moment. "This is the first time I got to kiss Mary Ellen and not KoKo," joked Rex.

It was a bit shocking to see how Rex had aged since I had met him less than ten years before in Tucson. It was also obvious that he was having very serious trouble with his vision, even though he was wearing heavily tinted glasses to conceal his eyes.

Rex, Virginia, Snuff, and Ellen were escorted by a security guard to a mobile home used for the celebrities to relax. Before she entered Ellen grabbed my hand and asked if I would please wait with her? I said I would. I must say that my love and respect for Ellen is such that there isn't much I wouldn't do for her anyway.

While waiting, the thing you couldn't help but notice is that Rex was a steady chain smoker. I can't remember a time at the festival, other than when he received his award and the Q & A session, that he didn't have a cigarette in his hand; it amazed me how strong his voice still was considering this.

It's interesting to look at Rex Allen's beginnings and notice how similar they are to Roy and Gene's. The odds of these three becoming singing cowboys of the silver screen must have seemed remote to them considering their rural upbringings. But the main thing they all had in common was a strong will to succeed...and on their own terms. It's a testament to their talents and fortitude that they made it all the way to the pinnacle of their craft.

I generally try to avoid giving an extensive childhood biography of stars; Rex's career however bears further examination to see how far talent and determination can take you. He made it to the top at a time when singing cowboys and the family 'programmer' western in general was on the way out.

Rex Elvie Allen was born as close to the end of 1921 as you could get, December 31, 1921, in Mud Springs, Arizona. His parents Horace and Fay raised cattle and goats; to help out Horace would play fiddle and call square dances.

Ellen: *"When Rex was a little boy of ten his father gave him a guitar. I think that when he gave Rex the guitar, he figured that Rex would go out on the road and accompany him."*

Rex: *"Many years ago, my dad was a bachelor and a good-looking guy. They were having this parade, (The Rex Allen Days Parade), and I came around this corner of the bank building on Koko with all this spangley (sic) stuff on waving at everybody. Dad was standing over on the corner with two or three old gals, and one of them said, 'Horace, I'll bet you're proud of that boy aren't ya?' He said, 'Yeah, I am proud of him.' She said, 'I wish I had a boy like that.' He said, 'Well, if you old girls hadn't been so damn persnickety a few years ago every damn one of you could have had one.'"*

In 1926, Rex's older brother Wayne was bitten by a rattlesnake and died two days later. It was at this time that the Allen family moved from Mud Springs to Willcox thirty-five miles away.

Anyone growing up in Willcox with Rex Allen would probably be lying if they ever said that they thought he would grow up to be a movie star. Poor, skinny and freckle faced, Rex had a more fundamental problem. He was terribly cross-eyed. Despite his physical problems, Rex persisted. He began to teach himself how to play the guitar and sing.

Ellen: *"Rex sang with school choirs, church choirs, glee clubs and after he graduated he landed a job with KOY, in Phoenix. Then he went to Trenton, New Jersey, where he became a singer and rodeo performer."*

After graduation from Willcox High School, in 1938, Rex went to Eastern Arizona Junior College and won a scholarship for his performance of *Lost in London Town*. With the help of the Willcox Rotary Club, Rex underwent corrective surgery to align his eyes; unfortunately, the surgery was a failure, but that didn't stop Rex.

He went on the rodeo circuit as a bronc buster. The tide really turned for him when he started singing cowboy songs billing himself as "Cactus Rex."

In Phoenix, Rex got the job at KOY where he talked program director Jack Williams, future Governor of Arizona (1967–1975), into letting him sing on the air. From there Rex moved to New Jersey where he got a big break at WTTM, not singing but reading commercial copy.

Rex: *"A station manager asked if I could read com-proceeded to mangle a commercial for cattle feed."*

Rex had never read a line of copy into a mike in his life but the station manager took pity on him.

Rex: *"The station manager handed me a bunch of old scripts and told me to 'go home, learn to talk and practice reading these.'"*

After mastering his speaking talents, and with his beautiful singing voice, Rex was discovered by a talent scout and invited to make an appearance on the National Barn Dance broadcast over WLS radio in Chicago.

It was here that he met a pair of singing sisters, Connie and Bonnie Linder. Rex fell for Bonnie and after a quick courtship they married.

During his time in Chicago, Rex honed his delivery and enunciation assisted by some of the top announcers of the day.

Rex: *"It was great training; I doubt that you can get that kind of help anymore."*

It was during his stint in Chicago, (1945-1949), that Rex successfully had his eye problem corrected. Using a local anesthetic, doctors lifted his left eyeball out of the socket, repaired the control cord, and then replaced it.

It was also now that Hollywood called for Rex. Herbert J. Yates, President of Republic Pictures, had lost Gene Autry, another alumnus of the National Barn Dance, to Columbia Pictures and Roy Rogers was "eyeing the door" (no pun intended) and so Yates needed a singing cowboy to replace them. The studio had signed Monte Hale a few years before Rex as a singing cowboy, but he proved to be no threat to either Gene or Roy; eventually Monte would continue at Republic as a non-singing cowboy. He would continue in film and television after his tenure at the studio in supporting roles. In 1956, Monte scored a very good role in George Steven's film, *Giant* starring Elizabeth Taylor, Rock Hudson, and James Dean.

Ellen: *"After he'd gone with Barn Dance, Herbert Yates, head of Republic Pictures, happened to hear his voice. Rex had turned down doing a movie playing a young 'Hopalong' Cassidy* (this is unconfirmed). *But then he made a few friends like Gene Autry and Roy Rogers and they talked him into thinking about it. After Herbert Yates called him and made him an offer he couldn't turn down he came out to Hollywood and from 1950 to 1954 he made nineteen movies. I'm very proud to say that I was in six of them."*

Rex: *"I was singing on a radio station in Chicago (WLS), and had some hit records goin', and Roy Rogers was leaving Republic Pictures to make his own series and do television. And Republic wouldn't allow any of their people to do television. They got to looking around for an idiot in a white hat...and I had the hat."*

Although most film histories say that Rex did 19 films for Republic Pictures, he actually did 20, including a guest stint in Roy Rogers' extravaganza *Trail of Robin Hood* (1950), along with Jack Holt, Allan "Rocky" Lane, Monte Hale, Tom Tyler, Ray "Crash" Corrigan, Kermit Maynard, Tom Keene and William Farnum.

To understand why Herbert J. Yates traveled all the way to Chicago to talk with Rex Allen, you need to understand what the climate at Republic Pictures was like in the late forties. To do that, however, we must go back even further to the Republic Pictures of the late thirties.

By 1937, Gene Autry was the number one cowboy star. In 1936, the first year of the Motion Picture Poll, he came in at number 3 with Buck Jones in the number one spot and George O' Brien as number two. It was now that tension between Gene and Herbert J. Yates reached its peak.

The studio had been growing rich off the Autry films, without giving Gene any raise along the way. Republic was also getting a percentage of his radio and personal appearance and endorsement fees as well. Because Autry was so popular, Republic was forcing exhibitors to buy as many as twelve non-Autry films of dubious quality to get eight Autry pictures. This form of 'Block Buying/Selling' was the last straw for Gene Autry; at least that's the way Gene wanted the public to perceive it. In reality it was a perfect ploy for a raise.

On the first day of shooting *Washington Cowboy* (1937) Gene sent word that he would not show up for work. Yates suspended Autry and sued him to prevent him from performing elsewhere or using his own name for any promotional purpose.

Yates had *Washington Cowboy* revamped to fit his new singing cowboy star, Roy Rogers and retitled it *Under Western Stars* (1938). To Yates pleasure both critics and audiences liked Rogers and a new star was born.

Because of Roy's immediate success, it was no surprise that soon after Autry and Yates came to terms. Gene would receive a raise but the package selling arrangement with theaters would continue. Autry's reign as the number one cowboy would remain intact through 1942, at which time he left to serve in the Army Air Corps.

Roy Rogers then officially became the 'King of the Cowboys' and would remain the number one cowboy star (on Top Ten Polls anyway) from 1943 through 1954, tying with Randolph Scott in 1953 and 1954, and coming in second to Scott in 1955. However, forevermore, people will argue who was the number one singing cowboy of all time, Gene or Roy.

During the time Autry was gone, Republic upped the budgets on Roy's pictures, making many of them into splashy musical productions with the action taking second place, all the while re-issuing Gene's films to prepare people for his eventual return to the studio. During this time, Autry continually came in second in the polls; no small feat considering these were not new pictures.

Herbert Yates loved the musical *Oklahoma* which debuted on stage in 1943. You'll notice that it was around this time that Roy's films began to feature gaudier musical numbers; also, a way of taking the audience's mind off the on-going war with lighter fare. Yates was so enamored with Broadway musicals that in 1938 he teamed Roy with contract player Lynne Roberts for a series of films changing her name to Mary Hart. In this way, Yates could bill them as "Rogers and Hart," to take advantage of the currently reigning stage musical writing team, Richard Rodgers and Lorenz Hart. Hart would die in 1943 and Rodgers then began his successful teaming with Oscar Hammerstein resulting in *Oklahoma*, based on the 1931 play *Green Grow the Lilacs*; However, I'm sure Yates had no thought of changing any of Roy's ingénue co-star's name to 'Hammerstein.'

When Gene Autry returned from his service in the Army Air Corp. he informed Yates that he would not be coming back to Republic Pictures;

instead he would be forming his own production company. Yates, however, had other ideas, telling Gene that he still owed the studio a contracted series of films not completed before leaving in 1942.

The deal was made for a final series of five films beginning with *Sioux City Sue* (1946). Smiley Burnette had already left Republic and was now under contract to Columbia Pictures as sidekick to Charles Starrett's 'Durango Kid' character. Yates would saddle Gene with the most ineffectual sidekick he could ever have, Sterling Holloway future voice of Disney's 'Winnie the Pooh.'

The war had matured Gene in looks and thoughts but Republic wanted the old Gene back as reflected in the final series of five films. This didn't set well with the singing cowboy and while settling his debt to Republic Pictures he made a deal with Columbia Pictures to release his independently produced films under the 'Gene Autry Productions' banner. As a final good-bye to Republic, Gene took much of the studio's production team with him.

Gene Autry released his first picture, *The Last Round-up*, in November of 1947, less than 4 months after his last for Republic, *Robin Hood of Texas*. The result was a grittier looking film with much more emphasis on action then music. The 'new' Autry fared better with audiences, however from his return to films in 1946 through 1954, he would rank number two in the polls and number five in the last poll taken in 1955, after George Montgomery in fourth place. But to be fair, Gene Autry would continue to beat Roy Rogers in song hits.

Monte Hale

In 1946, the same year Gene Autry returned to Republic, Yates hired another singing cowboy. No, not Rex Allen, he was still perfecting his craft on radio, recordings and live performances. The aforementioned Monte Hale would have the honor? becoming Republic's third singing cowboy.

Monte Hale started in support of Allan Lane, Robert Livingston, Richard Arlen, Bill Elliott, Sunset Carson, even Edward Everett Horton before moving on to his own series, starting with *Home on the Range* (1946).

Yates now had three singing cowboys at Republic ...but why? The answer may have been leverage against Gene and Roy. Yates had attempted to use Roy Rogers to leverage Autry in the thirties; it didn't really work, but Republic Pictures luckily found themselves with the two top singing cowboys as a result. Could lightning strike a third time? Unfortunately, the answer was "not quite yet."

Roy Rogers now firmly in the top spot at Republic, and the number one singing cowboy in films, was making demands of his own. With Gene Autry coming back to Republic, although not for long, Herbert J. Yates was probably worried about the demands these two top attractions would make on him.

Yates may have figured that a new singing cowboy, eager to please, would be just the ticket to keep Gene and Roy in line. After all, Yates could reason, "I made Autry and Rogers tremendous stars I could do it again." The only thing Yates didn't take into consideration was audience acceptance. Gene and Roy had personalities that jumped off the screen and grabbed their fans. Would Monte Hale be able to do that?

Yates gave Monte Hale a big build-up with color. *Home on the Range* was filmed in a cheap color process called Magnacolor, the process would be renamed Trucolor with his second film. Hale made six films in color, after that all his films were shot in black and white.

By this time, Autry had left Republic and Yates probably realized that Hale was not going to be a threat to Roy Rogers; Hale was the only Republic cowboy of any merit not to make the Top Ten list of cowboy stars.

In 1950, Monte Hale left Republic, but by then the search for a new singing cowboy had brought Herbert J. Yates to Chicago.

Rex: *"I got a call on Sunday morning at home saying that Mr. Yates wanted to talk to me, and I said, 'Who the hell is Mr. Yates?' Says he owns Republic Studios. I said, 'Yeah, I'll talk to him.' He got on the phone and wanted to know if I could come downtown and have breakfast with him at the hotel. So, I went down and visited with him. He asked me if I was interested in doing some pictures and I said, 'yeah.' So, I flew out there, spent three or four days, and they gave me a limo, and wined and dined me, and all that stuff, and I ended up signing a contract. No screen test, they just feel ya to see if you're warm."*

Rex would immediately become an asset in what would prove to be the waning days of the silver screen cowboy. With the mark, he made in the structure at Republic Pictures it's hard to believe that as he was coming in most of these cowpokes were defecting to television or retiring as leading "B" cowboy stars. Of the Republic stable Roy (on his way out) and Allan 'Rocky' Lane were the only permanent members left at the studio.

Starting with *The Arizona Cowboy* in 1950, through *Phantom Stallion* in 1954, Rex Allen would star in 19 pictures, plus guest-starring in *Trail of Robin Hood* (1950).

Rex: *"Our pictures were shot in about eight days. You had to run the horses fast, run yourself fast and, of course, the cameraman ran fast, and if you didn't get it in one take they were all mad at ya. So, we did it in one take."*

Singing and acting skills weren't the only things that Rex needed to prepare him to be a silver screen cowboy. One of the most important ingredients was still missing...his horse!

After all, Roy had Trigger and Gene had Champion! And let's not forget, Allan 'Rocky' Lane had Feather, and Black Jack aka Thunder, and Don Barry had Cyclone. Elsewhere, Ken Maynard had Tarzan, and Tom Mix had Tony. And, of course, The Lone Ranger had Silver (so did Sunset Carson).

Rex needed a horse for audiences to identify with. That horse was Koko. But what Rex didn't realize when choosing the right mount was that these screen horses had doubles to stand in for them.

Rex: *"Never did find a double for him and I hunted all over the world. They finally got to takin' a white horse and dying him with vegetable dye. Dyed off everything but his mane, tail, white socks, and the blaze in his face and it would last about seven or eight days, long enough; that's the only way we had a double for him.*

Rex and his 1st 'steady' sidekick, Buddy Ebsen

Koko was a real dark chocolate, almost black and white, and I must have bred him to 20 different mares thinking I'd get a double for him. About the time that the picture business was over, and I was working rodeos, I finally had a mare there that dropped a colt with a white mane and tail. He wasn't built like his daddy, but I had to turn Koko out to pasture for the last five years of his life, so I used his colt. We trained him and used him for about 5 years. Roy had a Trigger, Jr., Autry had a Champion, Jr. Looks like we outlived our horses!"

The other missing ingredient was a side-kick. Roy had Gabby and then Andy Devine, Gordon Jones, Pat Brady or...Ugh! Pinky Lee! Gene had Smiley at Republic, and later Pat Buttram (and Smiley) at Columbia. Rex needed a sidekick.

Gordon Jones, Carl "Alfalfa" Switzer and Fuzzy Knight appeared with Rex in his first films. But his movies really took off with *Under Mexicali Stars* (1950), when Buddy Ebsen took over sidekick duties.

By the time Ebsen came to Republic he had appeared on Broadway and in movies, opposite such stars as Shirley Temple. He also had an unfortunate stint as the original 'Tin Man' in *The Wizard of Oz*; due to a serious allergic reaction to the metallic paint used on him Ebsen was forced to leave the role. Jack Haley took over assuring him a place in film history.

Rex: *"It was a real pleasure and honor to work with Buddy Ebsen. Buddy had come out to the coast and we really lucked out getting him. He had been on Broadway and him and his sister were dancers. Buddy was a fantastic dancer, and a fine actor, and he was kind of starvin' to death or he wouldn't have been workin' at Republic. But they got him an old hillbilly suit, and a hat, and he made so much money that every pocket was full."*

Buddy Ebsen, of course, went on to television fame. After his sidekick days ended, he gained recognition as George Russel on Disney's *Davy Crockett* episodes for *Walt Disney Presents* (1954), and an Indian fighter on *Northwest Passage* (1958 & '59) He gained worldwide fame when he donned that "hillbilly suit and a hat," to become Jed Clampett on the long running *Beverly Hillbillies*. Following the success of *Hillbillies*, he went on to star in the popular television detective series, *Barnaby Jones*.

After Ebsen left Republic, Rex gained the sidekick that he is most associated with…Slim Pickens.

Rex: *"Slim Pickens was a rodeo clown before we gave him his first shot in his first picture."*

Rex and his best remembered sidekick, Slim Pickens

Ellen: *"I had this interview at Republic Studios that William Morris had set up for me, to meet Rex and (director) George Blair for a movie that they were shooting. I drove up to the gate and they let me in, and there was a bull corral and a bull was in it with Slim Pickens. Rex was standing there and it was such a sight! There was a barrel there and I watched Slim do a little exercise with the bull, and I remember Rex came over and made me feel so at ease."*

If you have ever seen *The Last Musketeer* (1951) with Rex, Ellen, and Slim then you've seen Slim perform one of his rodeo clown routines with a bull.

After his films at Republic, Slim went on to an extremely successful career in films and television. At the time of his death Slim Pickens was still in great demand.

Meanwhile, back at Republic, Rex Allen made the same number of pictures as Monte Hale had during his stay, but by his second year, 1951, Rex made the top ten list and stayed there through 1954. Yates had his successful new singing cowboy!

In 1951, after completing *Pals of the Golden West*, Roy Rogers left Republic to do his television show, this left Rex as their *only* singing cowboy.

Allan "Rocky" Lane

Things had changed greatly since Gene Autry had left in 1947. Gone was the large lineup of cowboy stars that made Republic the premier western studio. John Wayne had become a superstar and Gene, Roy and Dale Evans had gone into television; Bill Elliott had moved on to Monogram/Allied Artists, Don Barry to Lippert, and Sunset Carson to Yucca Productions/Astor Pictures, all low or no budget companies.

Judy Canova

By 1952, only Rex and Allan "Rocky" Lane, (who made a total of 51 films for the studio), were left under contract to Republic. Out of the two only Rex Allen consistently made the top ten from 1951 through 1954, although Lane's series of westerns remained of high caliber and still hold up quite well today. Republic contract player Judy Canova also made the top ten lists from 1951 through 1953 with her 'cornpone' western comedies for the studio.

Roy, Gene, Bill Elliott, Dale, Gabby, and Smiley also made it into the top ten during the early fifties, either through Republic re-issues, or films released by other studios.

By 1952, Rex was beginning to rival Roy's popularity, but the handwriting was on the wall. The 'programmer' westerns were dying. Established stars like George Montgomery, Randolph Scott, Joel McCrea, Glenn Ford, and Jimmy Stewart were making more 'adult' westerns, and actors like Audie Murphy and Rory Calhoun were changing the look of the 'B' western genre with sleekly produced studio product. And, of course, John Wayne was in a class by himself.

Charles Starrett

It would be up to Rex Allen and Allan "Rocky" Lane at Republic, Tim Holt at RKO, Gene Autry and Charles Starrett at Columbia, Lash LaRue at Western Adventures, and copycat Whip Wilson at Monogram, to ride the programmer trail into the 1950s.

Never given the credit he deserves, Charles Starrett started his western career at Columbia in 1935, releasing his last picture for them in 1952, (the last seven years playing the 'Durango Kid' exclusively), making him the only cowboy star to stay with his original studio through his entire western career of seventeen years.

Rex: *"You know Charles Starrett made more westerns then anybody who was ever in the business, and he was the only one who didn't come out broke. All the rest of us came out of there broke. Autry, and Rogers, and me, and all the rest of 'em. But Charlie Starrett was the heir to the Starrett Tool Corporation in Boston and if they didn't have the money to finance a picture Starrett gave it to them."*

At 134 full-fledged westerns in 16 years (although some were patched together from earlier series entries) it's no stretch to say Starrett not only holds the record for staying the longest at the same studio, and the largest amount of starring programmer westerns, but also to the most made in such a brief time...16 years. Gene made 93 films, including his time with Ken Maynard and two serials, 86 series films for Roy, not counting films in support of

Starrett, Autry, Tito Guízar, The Weaver Brothers and Elviry, or as a member of the Sons of the Pioneers; however Charles Starrett should be recognized as one of the greats of the western programmer, staying at the same studio, Columbia Pictures from 1935 through 1952, he scored the most 'oaters' with a total of 134 "B" westerns.

In 1954, Rex made his last film for Republic Pictures, *Phantom Stallion*, but Republic wasn't done with him yet. Television, once the enemy of movie moguls, was about to find a secret friend in Herbert J. Yates.

Just three years before Roy Rogers and Dale Evans left the studio…not under the best of circumstances…to hopefully star in their own television series.

Outwardly, Yates didn't want any of his contracted actors to have anything to do with this new threat to motion pictures, but there was a double standard going on. Yates was planning on selling the rights to Republic's library of western films to television stations, in doing so he would stand to make a bundle for himself at the expense of Republic's past and present stars.

But the whole aspect of working with television outlets produced a double-edged sword to the whole deal. If he had his past and present stars like Roy, Dale and Gene on television with their own shows then the major and independent station networks wouldn't pay top dollar for the Republic film library.

Likewise, he wanted them to remain under contract so that he could use their likenesses when promoting the sale of the film library as well as continuing with new product for the theaters. Gene was already gone and in full charge of his likeness and name, but Roy was still pending in negotiations and Rex and Allan Lane showed no sign of wanting to leave.

Dealing with the new "devil" known as television was a delicate quandary for Yates to place himself in. Republic Pictures faced the eventuality of closing its doors after the sale of their voluminous library of programmer westerns while bigger companies like Warner Bro. and Universal could eventually use the tie-in between television and film to benefit them and their leading contract players.

Bill Boyd saw the writing on the wall early on. He already owned rights to the Hopalong Cassidy series of film – both his and Harry Sherman's earlier productions except for the first one, *Hop-a-Long Cassidy (Enters)*.

Boyd had already begun to show his films on television in hour long truncated versions complete with commercials; eventually he would edit his later films to 30 minutes before beginning production on an original 30-minute TV show in 1952; with all the commercial tie-ins Boyd would make a fortune.

Duncan Renaldo and Leo Carrillo had been the last team to star in a series of films based on *The Cisco Kid* for United Artists and now were starring in a TV version as Cisco and Pancho; Frederick Ziv, producer of the series, had an eye for the future and wisely shot every episode in color.

Former Republic employee Gene Autry created a television empire in the early to mid-1950's under his television production banner 'Flying A Productions' by producing *Annie Oakley, Range

Rider, Buffalo Bill, Jr., and *The Adventures of Champion*; the company also filmed the pilot for a *Red Ryder* TV show starring Rocky Lane but it failed to attract a sponsor.

While Roy and Dale were willing to negotiate with Yates for a contract to continue at Republic for their films, they wanted it stipulated that they could also appear in their own television program. Yates was adamant on the fact that no Republic Pictures contract player would appear on television.

The result was Roy and Dale left Republic. *The Roy Rogers Show* did successfully appear on television, but not without legal problems from Yates. The whole story is told in my book, *Riding the Hollywood Trail II: Blazing the Early Television Trail*, but the result was that Herbert J. Yates tied Roy and Dale up in court for years resulting in a win for Yates in the fact that Republic Pictures retained rights to use their images when advertising the film packages sold to TV.

Furthermore, under their television releasing division, Hollywood Television Service, Yates and Republic would dabble in their own television productions; the 1953 serial *Commando Cody: Sky*

Marshal of the Universe was run in 1955 as a 12-episode television program and *The Adventures of Fu Manchu* (1956) were primary examples.

Rex in "Frontier Doctor"

Rex would eventually try his hand at a television series in 1958 with a vehicle a bit different for someone who had been known as a singing cowboy.

Ellen: *"I don't know if you knew this, but* Frontier Doctor *was Rex's idea."*

Rex: *"Yates didn't want anything to do with television, but he found out there was some money in it. I did a series called,* Frontier Doctor. *Shot 'em in two and a half days, two a week, for 39 episodes. I carried a little doctor bag that an old doctor in my hometown gave me and I carried that in the whole series. It wouldn't hold anything other than a hypodermic needle and a fifth of scotch."*

Frontier Doctor was not just a different step for Yates, and Republic Pictures, but a different type of western altogether. While Roy, Gene, and Hoppy rode the range, six guns blazing, Rex carried a 'well-supplied' medical bag. After *Frontier Doctor*, there would be sporadic on-screen appearances but a tremendous resurgence, and a whole new career path, was about to take place for as the saying goes: "When one door closes, another opens," and the door that opened was very lucrative indeed.

Rex: *"By the time I got to the west coast I had done a lot of commercial work in Chicago. Anyway, when I got to the west coast there was a party at Ciro's nightclub on the Sunset Strip. It's gone now, but somehow or other, my wife and I got seated at a table with Walt Disney and his wife. We talked for a long time and he said, 'Did you ever think about narrating films?' And I said, 'I don't know what you're talking about."* He said, *'Well, you just explain the scenes of film as they see 'em.' I said, 'You think I could do that?'" And he told me that he thought I could. He said, 'Next time it's handy for you drop by the studio, I'd like to talk to you about it.' I beat him down to the studio the next morning."*

Ellen: *"Rex wound up narrating over 150 episodes of Disney's Wonderful World of Color, and many of his features."*

Rex: *"I've done over a hundred of those over the years; it was a lot of fun. They just called me and my wife, and I went out there, and they gave me a Disney statue, and declared I was a 'Legend of Disney.' I'm nearly as big as Mickey Mouse."*

Ellen: *"He also narrated Hanna-Barbera's* Charlotte's Web. *I remember being in my kitchen and hearing a Purina Dog Chow commercial and thinking, 'There's Rex again!' That's how I've kept in contact with Rex through the years, by hearing his voice on all those commercials."*

From then on, besides singing engagements and recording, Rex Allen kept as busy as he wanted with his voiceover work; as a matter of fact he was scheduled for V.O. work on the day of his death.

Aside from his films and personal appearances, his successful recording career has given him hits such as the million selling *Crying in the Chapel*, which garnered him a gold record.

Up until Roy Rogers' death, Rex also kept in touch with his close friend from the Republic days. If there was ever a rivalry between Rex and Roy it was a friendly one.

In 1997, when I visited The Roy Rogers/Dale Evans Museum in Victorville, California, I got to talking with the manager who said that Rex would occasionally call Roy at the museum. "You can sure recognize that voice when he calls to talk with Roy,"

In 1982, Rex Allen, Jr. recorded his song, *The Last of the Silver Screen Cowboys*, in celebration of his famous dad. In the song, Rex, Sr. delivers some beautiful lines that recall quite vividly a time we will never be able to recapture. The innocence and excitement of the 1930s, '40s, and early '50s, when a kid could go to the neighborhood theater, sit in the dark, and watch Roy, Gene, Rex, and the rest, knowing that in little more than an hour the good guys might sing a few songs and prevail over Roy Barcroft, George Chesebro, or Kenne Duncan.

Ellen: *"Rex Allen is the last of that special Hollywood breed to crossover onto that beautiful silver screen, sitting on KoKo, strumming his guitar, and singing a beautiful western ballad. He's definitely the last of the Silver Screen Cowboys."*

Mary Ellen Kay said it all. Rex Allen arrived late as a singing cowboy. Roy Rogers had stopped making a regular picture series in 1951, and Gene had stopped making films at Columbia in 1953. Other singing cowboys like Tex Ritter, Monte Hale, Jimmy Wakely, and Eddie Dean had ceased production on their series westerns by 1949. Within one year of his arrival at Republic Pictures in 1950 Rex would be the last of the singing cowboys still making pictures there.

Earlier in this chapter I mentioned that Rex had brought Snuff Garrett with him to the Festival of the West. I also mentioned that Snuff had another purpose for being there and here's what it was:

It was obvious that during the Q & A session Rex was getting anxious to leave. At least twice he tried unsuccessfully to end the session with the pleased crowd and finally started inquiring as to where Snuff was. *"I hope he hasn't left, he has my car keys."*

He would then occasionally yell out, *"Snuff! Where's Snuff Garrett?"* while the audience and I tried to ask questions. Finally Snuff showed up. It turns out that *"Where's Snuff?"* was Garrett's cue to come in and take Rex away without too much furor. Snuff, however, had been looking around the festival and lost track of time and his purpose.

When Snuff finally showed up, Rex kindly but abruptly ended the interview and that was that. It was only later that I found out about their routine.

It was Mary Brown, owner of the Festival of the West, who would fill me in as to why he was so anxious to leave. *"He was a bit nervous, around so many people with his eye problems."* She told me that his vision was very limited and he felt uneasy around huge crowds. *"I recently went to breakfast with him, and he was wonderful to me,"* she added.

Now, with Gene and Roy gone, Rex Allen is indeed the Last of the Silver Screen *Singing* Cowboys, and if he had made it on the scene earlier who knows what might have happened. He had what it took to be a major rival to Roy and Gene. It's a tribute to his many talents that he left as large a mark as he did in such a short span of time at Republic Pictures.

Snuff Garrett (standing) with a few other "B" stars. Left to right sitting: Colonel Tim McCoy, Kirk Alyn (first Superman in serials), Monte Hale, Roy Rogers. Sitting on far right is "Tomorrow Show" host, Tom Snyder

The whole scenario surrounding *"Where's Snuff?"* is funny to me now and it's is a phrase I'll blurt out in uneasy situations when someone is around who knows what I'm talking about. It's a great laugh and a terrific remembrance.

It's fitting to leave you with the last words of Rex's 1998 Cowboy Spirit Award speech; I imagine it sums up the feelings of all true cowboy film fans as well.

Rex: *"I hope you all live a thousand years and I never die."*

Update:

Unfortunately, Rex Allen's untimely passing from coronary problems came the very next year on December 17, 1999, two weeks before his 79th birthday. While waiting for his assistant to pull his car out of the garage and into the driveway, he collapsed behind the car. As the car was backed out Rex went unnoticed until the vehicle backed over him. Rex was unconscious at the time. It's believed the heart attack had already caused his death.

He was cremated and his ashes were scattered at Railroad Park across from the Rex Allen Museum in Willcox, Arizona. One of my many treasured

Two Legends...Rex Allen and Roy Rogers

mementoes is a cassette recording of Rex singing Led Zeppelin's *Stairway to Heaven*.

"The Last of the Silver Screen Cowboys" recording session. Left to right: Rex Allen, Jr., Rex Allen, Sr., Roy Rogers.

In closing one of my favorite stories that exemplifies Rex Allen's sense of humor is the time he got into an elevator already occupied by a lady who became awestruck at the sight of the singing cowboy is was solely sharing the elevator with. She did manage to get out a few words:

"I am such a fan...I love your voice and your movies...it would be an honor to have your autograph, Mr. Rogers."

Without missing a beat, Rex took her pen and paper and jotted down his 'autograph,' which said, *"I appreciate you being such a huge fan, but I'll never be the singer that Rex Allen is. Happy Trails, Roy Rogers."*

CHAPTER 3
Harry Carey, Jr.
Reminiscing about Harry Sr., John Wayne, John Ford, Ben Johnson & the Career of a Supporting Player

To western film fans Harry Carey, Jr. is part of a film history dynasty. His father was a major film star, his mother a well-known actress in the movie community and his father-in-law, a successful character actor. In his career, he's ridden the range with John Wayne and Ben Johnson, been a part of John Ford's stock company and appeared on stage with me! Well, maybe the stage appearance is no big deal, but since his film debut in *Rolling Home* (1946) with Russell Hayden, Harry "Dobe" Carey, Jr. has had a successful career in film and television.

From *Red River* to *Tombstone* on the big screen, to Disney's *Spin & Marty* and *Moochie of the Little League* on TV, he carries on the family legacy. "It's a business," he told me in 1984, when we appeared on stage together in *Mr. Roberts*. "I'm lucky because I don't have to carry the picture. I come in and do my part and then I move on to the next job."

He also finds it amusing that he doesn't always get his due from the film community.

"When I showed up on the set of Tombstone, *to play Fred White, Dana Delany (Josephine Marcus) came up to me and started going on about how much she respected me and enjoyed my work. Later-on, I found out that she thought I was Harry Caray, the sports announcer. When she found out I wasn't, she wasn't quite as friendly towards me; I think she spent some time trying to figure out just who I was."*

Ben Johnson, the author, and Harry Carey, Jr.

It wasn't the only time that would happen. In 1995, when Harry Carey, Jr. was to receive the Cowboy Spirit Award at the National Festival of the West, the Phoenix based Arizona Republic newspaper ran a picture of the sports announcer instead.

Dobe Carey takes it all in stride with a good sense of humor. To prove the point, here's an incident that happened at the 1994 festival:

Dobe and his good friend Ben Johnson were asked to present the Cowboy Spirit Award that year to Gene Autry. Who better to give the award to such a giant of the western screen than two other giants of the genre? They both took their turns at the mic, talking about the famous singing film star and then presented the award to Mr. Autry. Gene slowly walked out on stage, using a cane to steady himself. He accepted the award, thanking Dobe and Ben, and then proceeded to hold the audience in the palm of his hand as he talked about his career for the better part of an hour. All too quickly it was over and the the fragile star was helped off stage.

After the presentation, I walked backstage to say *"Hi"* to Dobe, who I had not seen since our stage appearance together ten years before. As I entered the backstage area I'll never forget the scene. There was Dobe sitting in a chair with Ben standing over him. They were debating about whether Gene Autry even knew who they were…

"I don't think he knew me, but I think he knew you," Ben said.

"I don't think so, but he seemed to know who you were," Dobe shot back.

"No…he knew you because of your dad," Ben said

"But you won the Oscar" was Dobe's reply

This exchange continued until I stepped in to say my 'hello.' Imagine these two respected actors, one of them an Academy Award winner, arguing whether Gene Autry knew who they were? This is how unassuming stars like Harry Carey, Jr. and Ben Johnson are (were).

When I reminded Dobe of this scene in 1998, he laughed and then explained why he felt that way.

Dobe: "*Gene and Roy grew up watching my father, and they would always yell, 'Oh, that's Harry Carey's boy!' You know, here I am with a white beard and 77 years old, but I'm still Harry Carey's boy to those guys.*"

Harry Carey, Sr.

(This remark was made in March of 1998. Just months before Roy (July 6th, 1998) and then Gene (October 2nd, 1998 would leave us).

I can't think of an actor I respect more than Dobe. Because of this, I won't spend much time talking about the stories he related to me concerning the John Ford Stock Company or about his family and career. You can read about those things in his fascinating autobiography, *Company *of Heroes: My Life with the John Ford Stock Company*, a must read for any film fan. It includes how he got the nickname "Dobe" (pronounced Dobie). So, unless you've attended a festival where he was, know him personally, or have read his book already, you'll just have to get the book to find out his nickname's origin.

My first memories of Dobe are not from *3 Godfathers* (1948) or *She Wore a Yellow Ribbon* (1949), but from the *Spin & Marty* serial on the *Mickey Mouse Club*. While most boys my age were relating to Spin or Marty, two boys who meet at a boy's ranch and have all sorts of adventures, I was interested in Bill Burnette, the ranch counselor. I didn't know who the actor was who played him, but his easy-going manner impressed me even as a kid.

Whenever I saw the actor I would think to myself, *"Hey, there's the Spin & Marty guy!"* It wasn't until I was older that I put a name to the face. *"Harry Carey? What kind of a name is that?"* I thought that was a way some Japanese guy killed himself. I had no idea of the history that named carried.

Dobe: *"1909 was when my dad started in movies, back in Fort Lee, New Jersey. He was John Wayne's idol, you know? John Wayne had a very short attention span. If you didn't get it out in about 30 seconds, his eyes started wandering around. But once, when we were working on 'The Undefeated' in 1968 he came up to me and wanted to reminisce.*

"I had made 11 or 12 films with him and he wanted to talk about my father. He talked about how, when he was a young guy, he couldn't stand the way he moved, or couldn't stand to watch himself on the screen, and so he took a lot of my dad's mannerisms which fit him.

I never looked like my father, Duke looked more like a son of my father then I did. Duke, by the way, told me when I was getting started that I should get out of pictures because I wasn't handsome enough and too skinny and he was about half right."

Dobe also married into an acting family. His beautiful wife, Marilyn, is the daughter of the well-known character actor, Paul Fix, best known for playing lawman Micah on *The Rifleman* with Chuck Connors despite appearing in countless films and television programs, before and after…well over 300 credits to be as exact as possible.

Dobe: *"My father-in-law had a face everybody knew. He used to play gangsters in the old days. He's a wonderful actor, played Elizabeth Taylor's father in 'Giant.' He also taught John Wayne how to do that walk of his. Like I said, Duke was unhappy with the way he came across on screen and Marilyn's father showed him how to point his*

Paul Fix

toes inward to get that walk that he became famous for."

The first time I could see Dobe in the flesh was in the late 1970s. I was working on a television show in Salt Lake City when it was announced that a western film festival would be held at a local theater; filmmaker Peter Bogdanovich was going to be there to interview Harry Carey, Jr. about the western films of John Ford.

It was an exciting weekend for me. Not only did I sit through 16 hours of western films, but I was front and center for the interview with Harry Carey, Jr. It was interesting and informative, a perfect way to cap off the festival. Little did I know that within a few years I would be working on stage with him!

It was 1984 and the announcement was made that Harry Carey, Jr. would be coming to the Promised Valley Playhouse in Salt Lake City to play the Captain in *Mr. Roberts*. I had been doing quite a bit of stage work at the playhouse and I really was anxious to do this play due to Dobe being a part of the cast. I knew the director, Joanne

Parker, very well and felt confident that I would secure the part of "Ensign Pulver," the movie role that Jack Lemmon received an Academy Award for.

In the original movie, James Cagney played the Captain and, of course, Henry Fonda played Roberts, and Dobe played one of the sailors (Stefanowski) on the ship. Add to this, the fact that William Powell, Ward Bond, Nick Adams, Phillip Carey, Ken Curtis, and Patrick Wayne were also in the cast and that the film was co-directed by Mervyn LeRoy and John Ford, and you have a lot of Hollywood history...much of it in the western genre.

Well, I'd like to say that I got the part of Pulver, but, I didn't. I was devastated and I can't tell you how many times I picked up the phone to call the director to tell her that I wouldn't do the play. But still, I thought no matter what part I had, I would still be able to act on the same stage with Harry Carey, Jr. and hopefully talk with him about the "Duke," John Ford and all the rest of the legends he had worked with. Better judgement prevailed and I accepted the part of "Wiley," one of the sailors,

(Tige Andrews, Captain Greer on *The Mod Squad*, played Wiley in the film) and am I glad that I did.

It was a terrific experience. Dobe was wonderful to us all and, when he wasn't on stage, he would answer my questions. I'm sure he would rather have been concentrating on his part, but he was a true gentleman.

I also found that during rehearsals, if I added little pieces of improvisation here and there Joanne would tell me to leave it in. It got to the point where my role was becoming as large as that of Pulver.

The role was even more rewarding when a newspaper critic's review for the show singling me out saying that I could "get away with things other actors would fall flat on their faces trying to do." This was made even more enjoyable when the critic went on to give the actor playing Pulver a terrible review. I think the icing on the cake was when the director told me that Dobe had taken her aside and told her that I should have played Pulver. I was in hog heaven to think that Harry Carey, Jr. would have said that about me.

Now here it was 1994, and word got to me that Dobe would be at the National Festival of the West. I dug out a picture of the two of us taken at the *Mr. Roberts* cast party. I was sure he wouldn't remember me, after all he had done many many more important roles in film and television since then, so why would he remember me? I planned to wait until the celebrity panel Q & A I would commandeer and then show the picture to him; maybe talk a little about the experience and then go on with more important questions.

Imagine my disappointment on the first day of the Q & A sessions when I was told that Dobe wouldn't be participating in any panels during that day. However, I knew that the next day he would be presenting the Cowboy Spirit Award, along with Ben Johnson, to Gene Autry with a Q & A session to be held right after the award ceremony. I figured I could wait until then.

The next day came; Dobe and Ben gave the award to Gene Autry. Gene gave his acceptance speech and then left. It was now time for the Q & A and with picture in hand I was ready. My friend, Hank Sheffer, who handled main-stage presentations, then came out to give me the sad news. Dobe wouldn't be taking part in that day's sessions either! Hank told me that he would take me backstage so that I could at least say *"Hi"* to Dobe.

Disappointed, I figured it was better than nothing so off we went. Later I found out I could have been back-stage to meet Gene, but in the early days of my panel moderating duties I felt like I was intruding when I did that. When we got backstage the first thing I saw was the scene I mentioned earlier between Dobe and Ben arguing about whether Gene Autry knew who they were or not.

Hank took me up to Dobe and started to reintroduce me to him, "Dobe, I have somebody here who would like to say *'Hi'* to you. You remember...."

At this point, I interrupted Hank to avoid any embarrassment on either Dobe's part or mine. Of course, he wouldn't remember me. Why should he? I quickly held out my hand and said: *"Dobe, you won't remember me, but we did "Mr. Roberts" together in Salt Lake City."* To which Dobe quickly added, *"And you should have played Pulver!"*

You could have knocked me over with a dove feather! He remembered! He told me to sit down. I did, and we had a terrific conversation. I told him that I was doing the Q & A moderating and just wanted to say 'hello' because I heard that he wasn't staying for it. He looked surprised: *"Nobody asked me to stay, I didn't know anything about it, but if you're doing it I'll stay!"* He did, and he came back to the festival every year until health prevented him.

Harry Carey, Jr. is the type of actor that makes any film he's in a bit better or at least bearable… such as *Billy the Kid Meets Dracula*, (1967) in which his mother, Olive Carey, also appeared; her last film in a career that started in 1912.

To quote another popular actor and friend, Buck Taylor: *"It seems to me, we don't have too many character actors to speak of. There's a few, but not like in the old days when we had a stable of character actors that fit into certain areas and you looked forward to seeing them, because they were like the defensive line of a football team. They made the good guys look better than they were sometimes."*

Addition: Since saying this in 1997, Buck Taylor has comfortably eased into becoming one of those welcome 'character actors.'

Buck's own father, Dub, was one of those; so were Denver Pyle, Strother Martin, L.Q Jones, Slim Pickens, Jack Elam, and George Kennedy, but nobody worked any harder than Dobe. We can turn on the TV and watch his acting skills mature and grow right before our eyes. From playing the naive doomed boy of *The 3 Godfathers* to the more heroic friend in *Wagonmaster* we believed him. He then progressed gracefully to the wise father figure of *Spin and Marty*, and onto the grizzled character actor of such film classics as *Two Rode Together* and *Tombstone*, and we believed him. That's Harry Carey, Jr.'s strength, his characters always ring true. But growing old "gracefully" doesn't come without its drawbacks, as Dobe will tell you.

Dobe: *I was working with Hugh O' Brian a few years ago on some terrible thing* (Return to Tombstone), *where he reprised his Wyatt Earp* *role; it was awful. Hugh is really deaf. I mean, he is so deaf that I kept greeting him and he wouldn't answer me. He comes in and I'm supposed to say something like, "Why, it's Wyatt Earp," and he never heard me. Finally, I started waving at him when we started doing the scenes together. It was bad, because I was deaf and he was deaf.*

Dobe is one of a kind. He's respected and in great demand in an industry that is known for using and abusing its own. He's not just a survivor, but a clear winner and I'm truly proud to know him and call him a friend. The following are some excerpts from my 1998 interview with Dobe.

On John Ford: *He could be a scary guy. Ford would only get nasty if he didn't think you were giving him one hundred percent. Being a young actor, you'd think you were being the best that you could be and he'd look at you like it was amateur night in Dixie. But he was a great director and I gotta tell you something, I loved him like a dad.*

In Dobe's book, *Company of Heroes*, he mentions that John Ford would threaten to replace him with Audie Murphy. I asked him why?

Dobe: *I worked with Audie twice. I did a test with him for John Huston about 50 years ago and then I worked with him on a TV show at Universal (Whispering Smith-1961). He was a terrific guy. Audie, admittedly, wasn't too proud of his own acting; he just never thought he was much of an actor.*

Now, I don't know whether John Ford thought he was a good actor or a bad actor but every time I'd screw up Ford would say to me, "Audie Murphy begged me for this part.

Ford kept saying that and I wanted to quit. After about three days of this John Wayne took me aside and told me that Ford kept throwing Gary Cooper at him.

Wayne said that when he was playing the Ringo Kid, in Stagecoach, *John Ford would tell him, "I wish I had Gary Cooper, 'cause you're really screwin' this up!" But Audie was a tough little guy, he wouldn't fisticuff with anybody, he'd just shoot* ya! You didn't want to get on the wrong side of him."

(As a sidenote, whatever John Ford thought of Audie Murphy, at least one major director thought highly of him. John Huston used Murphy in two films, *The Red Badge of Courage* (1951) and *The Unforgiven* (1960), both proving that he really could act.)

Dobe continued:

I did one Gunsmoke a year, but here's something you may not know. I tested for the part of Chester with Raymond Burr, who was being considered for the part of Marshal Dillon.

Audie Murphy

As I said at the beginning of this chapter, there's a lot that I could talk about concerning Harry Carey, Jr. and our time together. I could tell you more about Harry Carey, Sr., John Ford, John Wayne, and Dobe's very good friend, Ben Johnson, but much of it is in his book, *Company of Heroes*. It's a great read and Dobe tells it better than I ever could.

I look forward to my next meeting with Harry Carey, Jr. You're a great man Dobe and I'm proud to know you. I must close this chapter now, *Spin and Marty* is coming on the Disney Channel.

Harry Carey, Jr. & Roy Barcroft in "Spin & Marty"

Addendum:

Dobe passed away on December 27th, 2012. Unfortunately, I hadn't seen him or been in contact with him for the last decade of his life. In March of 1998, on the opening day of The Festival of the West, I presented him with a copy of this book. I had just gotten the published book and hadn't had a chance to look at it myself. The next day at the festival he came up to me and gave me a positive thumb up concerning his chapter in the book with a very nice, "Thank-you."

He's gone now, but I hope he's looking down and listening when I say, "No, Dobe…thank-you."

CHAPTER 4
Lash LaRue

Did Your Mother Ever Meet Humphrey Bogart
Don Barry Sees "Red"
& "Fuzzy was Fuzzy!"

The first year of The National Festival of the West, I was involved in producing some television segments about the festival for a program called, *The Arizona Cowboy*. At that time, I wasn't doing any of the celebrity interviews at the festival; that was handled by a very talented Phoenix film critic and movie host, Bill Rocz.

Even though it was the first year, Mary Brown and her crew at the event did a bang-up job, and the roster of talent they had was quite good. John Smith (*Laramie*), Jan Merlin (*The Rough Riders*), Randy Boone (*The Virginian*) and screen legend Lash LaRue, were on hand to meet their fans.

The only star I met that year was John Smith, even though Lash's booth was right next to his. I guess I was just so awestruck and cautious because of his reputation as being temperamental, that I couldn't bring myself to talk to him.

I had read a lot about his temperament and his escapades off the screen and really didn't know what to make of him. To tell the truth, even after I met him and had a chance to interview him the following year, I still didn't know what to make of Al 'Lash' LaRue.

The first Festival of the West at Rawhide in 1991. Far left: Randy Boone (The Virginian), Center Jan Merlin (The Rough Riders) on stage coach, John Smith (Laramie).

Lash had a way of staring at you and making you feel uncomfortable. According to those who knew him, that was his way of sizing you up, but I didn't know that at the time and it made me feel very uneasy; I'm sure he felt the same when he caught me staring at him

That first year I would pass his booth and he would just stare at me; no smile...no "Hi Partner," just a stare. I didn't know what to make of him, and frankly it set me on edge. So, the 1991 festival came and went, and Lash LaRue moved on to his next appearance.

By 1991 Lash was ill and would stop making appearances after 1993; with his 1992 and final Festival of the West appearance I would have my only chance to meet and interview him. There's so much that I have learned about him since that interview, I wish I had just one more festival with him, but that, as we know can never be...at least not in this life.

Sunset Carson

Lash LaRue and Sunset Carson were probably more instrumental than any other cowboy film stars in popularizing these western festivals. Starting in the late 1970's the western festivals started to gather steam and Lash and Sunset attended as many of them as they could, making most of their income from the merchandise sold at these events. That they made a living off the festival circuit is understandable since both Lash and Sunset had what would be considered successful but brief western film careers.

Both were limited in their appeal and acting ability, although Sunset Carson did make the Motion Picture Herald Poll of Top Ten Western Stars in 1946; Lash, surprisingly, never did make it onto the Herald or Box-office polls, the two major film polls of the time. Looking over the western polls from 1945 through 1951, sidekicks like Fuzzy Knight, Leo Carrillo, Andy Devine, Smiley Burnette, and Gabby Hayes were making the top ten; popular sidekicks, but sidekicks none the less, however, no Lash LaRue.

Sunset Carson even had Republic Pictures behind him while Lash was a product of the lowest film producer of Gower Gulch, Producer's Releasing Corporation (PRC); so, it might come as a surprise to some hard-core fans to find that Lash LaRue's name, if not the actor himself, is more familiar to passing fans of the genre than silver screen cowboys from the much larger stable of Republic Pictures such as Sunset Carson, Allan "Rocky" Lane and Don "Red" Barry.

The name, Lash LaRue, probably has a lot to do with it. While many baby boomers are familiar with the name, few have probably ever seen him or his movies, and those who have most likely remember him more for the black outfit, the whip and his physical resemblance to actor Humphrey Bogart than anything else.

Sunset has been described to me by one of his former leading ladies, Peggy Stewart, as: "big, cute, and cuddly." as a matter of fact, Mary Brown told me *"Sunset was one of the kindest, sweetest, dearest men I ever met."* On the other hand, Lash was compact and mysterious; an anti-hero in films before anyone had ever heard of Clint Eastwood or Lee Van Cleef.

The biggest drawback to the career of Al "Lash" LaRue may have been his striking resemblance to Humphrey Bogart, a star of the first magnitude; upon meeting LaRue, character actress Sarah Padden asked if LaRue and Bogie were related? When Al said, he didn't think so, Padden slyly asked, "Did your mother ever meet Humphrey Bogart?"

LaRue was not bad looking, he couldn't help having that 'Bad Boy' look some women loved, it's just that he reminded producers of Humphry Bogart in looks and voice. It's probably safe to say that some actors such as Lash LaRue may not have become western stars if they hadn't looked so much like already established actors, thereby ruining their chance for mainstream stardom.

Don 'Red' Barry, a very fine actor, would probably have had a good career in other genres, and indeed strived for that chance diligently. If it hadn't been for the fact that he looked and acted so much like James Cagney he might have made it.

Al LaRue would have probably had a nice career in gangster films if it had not been for the fact that he looked, sounded, and acted so much like Bogie. Comparing the careers of both Donald Barry and Al LaRue, actors who both suffered from their similarities to bigger stars, is interesting in the paths they both took.

Barry's career as a Republic western star was relatively brief. Starting in movies in 1933, Barry appeared in 25 films including a recurring character in the Dr. Kildare series at MGM, before signing at Republic Pictures where he appeared in support of the Three Mesquiteers, and Roy Rogers before starring in his first western vehicle for the studio, *Ghost Valley Raiders* in 1940. That same year he starred as the title character in the 12-chapter serial *The Adventures of Red Ryder*, the film that would forever label him with a nickname he detested, "Red." From then until his his final starring western for the studio, Outlaws of Santa Fe (1944) Barry starred or supported stars like Roy Rogers in 29 westerns for Republic. Along the way, the studio placed him in a few non-genre films usually of the Cagney mold, billed Donald Barry.

Barry left his spurs and horse, for the most part, behind after his guest star role in the Roy Rogers' all-star-extravaganza *Bells of Rosarita* in 1945, much to the pleasure of crew and Republic contractees. It's been said that Barry had an unbridled ego and once had a sidekick fired because he was taller than the slight star - director William Witney referred to him as "the midget." He would remain on the western top ten lists through 1945.

Remaining at Republic until 1948 he would be billed as Donald Barry in a few westerns in supporting roles with Roy Rogers and Bill Elliott, as well as a handful of non-western genre films that continued to remind people of just how much he reminded them of James Cagney.

Along with the later Allan 'Rocky' Lane series Barry's early to mid-1940s westerns hold up very well and it's a shame he wouldn't stick around for a few more; as it was, by the time he left the genre he had already been typecast.

Republic seemed to take great pains in showing just how good he was, with interesting storylines that showcased his acting skills, often having him playing more than one part within the hour's adventure. He was Republic's 'Thinking Man's Cowboy Star.'

It's a shame he couldn't have had a mind-set like William Elliott who easily and gladly switched from his "B" series films billed as 'Wild Bill' Elliott to a Republic "A" film as 'William Elliott.'

Don "Red" Barry

But Barry grew dissatisfied with his career in westerns and was very hard to work with; Republic Studio director John English finally refused to work with him.

He tried, unsuccessfully, to break out of the mold, and thus shortened his successful career and chances at Republic Pictures. When he realized it, it was too late, although he would continue as a supporting player for decades.

Al "Lash" La Rue, on the other hand, seemed resigned to the fact that he would forever be known as a western hero. While Barry grew bitter about his career as he drifted in and out of westerns, usually in small supporting roles that took advantage of his past association with the genre, Lash relished the limelight as the 'Bad Boy' of the programmer westerns.

Of the two, Don Barry had much more going for him. His acting skills where top notch, and the production values of his Republic films were very high. His legacy at the number one cowboy studio should have been secure, but Barry wanted more than a career as a highly recognizable cowboy star.

Lash, on the other hand, was limited in his potential appeal. The shoddy production values of studios like Producers Releasing Corporation would have sunk a man of lesser determination; Buster Crabbe left PRC's successful 'Billy Carson' series hoping to move on to better things – his fans can be the judge of whether he made it or not - but Lash LaRue if nothing else was determined to be a success, even at the bottom of the production food chain.

After leaving Republic, Barry would find his way back to the western trail in 1949, releasing a series of pictures through Lippert Pictures. Founded by Robert Lippert, an owner of a chain of second run movie houses, the studio was formed to fight the major studios and their exorbitant rental fees and block selling practices. Originally known as Screen Guild Productions, Lippert's first release was a 1945 cinecolor western called *Wildfire* with a strong supporting cast including Eddie Dean, Gene Alsace (Rocky Camron), Sarah Padden Francis Ford (John's older brother), and William Farnum with Sterling Holloway thrown into the mix for 'comedy?'

In 1948, SGP became Lippert Pictures, not really a studio at all but a production house using rental stages and exteriors such as Corriganville. It was successful enough to release 130 features between 1948 and 1955, using well-known actors like Veronica Lake, Robert Alda, Preston Foster, Zachery Scott, Gloria Jean, Jack Holt, Ellen Drew, Sabu and Donald Barry

The first two for Barry would be *Ring Side* and *The Dalton Gang*, both in 1949 and both produced for Lippert by Ron Ormond who was already producing Lash LaRue and Al 'Fuzzy' St. John's films for his independent company, Western Adventures, since PRC let the duo go in 1947.

Three of his last four last four for Lippert, *Gunfire*, *I Shot Billy the Kid*, and *Train to Tombstone* were billed as Donald Barry Productions; he then starred and directed a United Artists' release with the enticing title, *Jesse James Women* (1954). All of these were a far cry from his days at Republic; although he tried to fight using the nickname in his billing there's plenty of publicity showing his films being hyped starring Don 'Red' Barry.

Although terribly shoddy productions, Barry's personality was strong enough to make them usually seem better than they were, although none hold up to inspection today like his Republic output.

Don Barry would never regain his halcyon days at Republic and after a life of unrealized dreams Donald Barry ended it all on July 11, 1980 after a domestic dispute. I was very sad when I heard the news of his passing. He was, and still is, one of my favorites. Barry is one actor that I enjoy watching over and over, and I always love talking to people who knew and worked with him, like Peggy Stewart who literally worked with every "B" western actor in Hollywood during their heyday except one...Don Barry. Instead she married him for a brief spell; it lasted as long as Don's western film series for Republic, 1940 – 1944, although I doubt that had anything to do with the divorce...or did it?

Al LaRue didn't ever have a studio like Republic behind him. His films, at best, can only be termed adequate but he made the best of what he was given to work with and was grateful for it.

Lash: *I wasn't bothered with being typecast in westerns. Ever since I was a kid I dreamed of being a cowboy because they were respected. My heroes growing up were people like Tom Mix and Ken Maynard.*

LaRue had a stubborn determination to survive in the genre fate had guided him to and, with his black outfit, cocked hat and whip, he catapulted himself into a cowboy legend.

Alfred LaRue was born in Gretna, Louisiana on June 14, 1916. A meeting with Warner Bros. contract player, George Brent, would take young Al away from college in Stockton, California, and change his life forever.

Brent arranged for a screen test at Warner Bros. for Al, probably not the best studio to take him for a screen test since Warner's already had Bogart under contract.

a screen test since Warner's already had Bogart He didn't get a contract with Warner Bros. but he decided he might like the life of an actor and started making the rounds at all the studios and finally was signed by Universal Pictures. However, after a couple of films in small roles, Universal dropped him from their roster.

What possibly seemed like a bad break at the time was good fortune for Al. If Universal hadn't dropped him, he might never have entered the 'gates,' such as they were, at Producers Releasing Corporation.

Robert Tansey was looking for an actor to play a character known as "The Cheyenne Kid" in an Eddie Dean western called *Song of Old Wyoming* (1945). The only catch was that the character was skillful with a bullwhip, something Al was not, but he didn't let that 'small' matter stop him.

Lash: *Tansey told me that he had intended to use a guy who could use a whip, and I told him that I had been using one since I was a kid.*

Al lied about being proficient with the whip and won the role...it does seem a bit odd that PRC simply took his word about his expertise with a whip; eventually he admitted to Tansey that he couldn't use a whip at all.

Lash: *The whip had been hanging on my gun for the first few days of shooting when Tansey came up to me and said he wanted to use me on my own series at three times what I was getting paid working in the Eddie Dean pictures. It was then that I thought I'd better tell Bob that I couldn't really use a whip. Tansey was a little upset, but I said to him, 'Look, Bob, you doubted that I could act, but you believed me when I told you that I could use a whip.' He laughed and hired a guy* (Snowy Baker) *to teach me how to use a whip and I became pretty good at it.*

Mary Brown told me that she had seen Lash use a whip in his final years and he wasn't boasting when he said that he could use it.

Song of Old Wyoming, starring Eddie Dean, was considered a prestige piece for PRC, in that it was filmed in a cheap color tint process called Cinecolor. Today however instead of being known as Eddie Dean's first color western, *Song of Old Wyoming*, may be better known as the movie that introduced Al LaRue to western fans.

Eddie Dean

Al stole the picture from Dean and the fan mail started pouring into the offices at PRC. It was obvious that western fans wanted more of the cowboy dressed in black. According to Dean, he suggested to Tansey that Al should have his own series. This could be quite possible, considering that Dean might have wanted to get rid of any competition in his own films considering he had waited far too long for a big break to be upstaged by this young 'whip'er snapper.

Edgar Dean Glosup was born on July 9, 1907, in Posey, Texas. Although Eddie Dean will never be in the same category as the Republic singing stars; Roy, Gene and Rex, he could arguably be the most successful independent singing cowboy, except for Tex Ritter; Jimmy Wakely could make claim as well.

Dean starred in twenty features while at PRC. For three years, Dean rode the celluloid range, making the top ten lists in 1946 and 1947.

It's probably safe to say that Dean did not want to share his moment in the sun with the likes of Al LaRue.

Al LaRue was not in Dean's second color western; he had been killed at the end of *Song of Old Wyoming*. But that didn't stop Tansey from bringing Al back in the third film of the series, *The Caravan Trail* (1946), this time as a character named "Cherokee" and Dean's fifth and final Cinecolor film, *Wild West* (1946) as the character "Stormy Day." All three of his supporting roles in Eddie Dean vehicles were released on a very leisurely schedule, October 1945 – December 1946.

To say that Al was quickly placed into his own series just isn't true, considering the time frame of Republic stars of the same time. LaRue didn't appear on the screen again until the tail end of February in his own

Buster Crabbe

series using the moniker, 'Cheyenne Davis.'

The departure of PRC's most popular cowboy, Buster Crabbe, in September 1946 also left a hole in their "B" westerns that needed filled. Impressed with the amount of fan mail Al had been getting, PRC felt that he was the logical choice to promote to his own series.

By this time, Al LaRue had become an expert with the bullwhip so PRC started to bill their new star as Al "Lash" LaRue, occasionally dropping the Al altogether.

Al "Fuzzy" St. John

He would inherit Buster's regular sidekick and Al couldn't have been given anyone better than another Al, Al "Fuzzy" St. John.

On their teaming, Lash had this to say: *Fuzzy didn't like me very much when we started. He had gotten it in his mind that I had something to do with Buster leaving the studio. Anyway, we worked together for nearly a year before he told me that at the start of our teaming he made up his mind he wasn't going to like me. It took him almost a year to realize that I was an okay guy. After that, we became good friends.*

Beginning with *Law of the Lash* (1947), Lash LaRue would play the part of "Cheyenne Davis" in eight films for PRC; after the eight he would drop the name and simply go by Lash LaRue

In 1948, Lash and Fuzzy moved to producer Ron Ormond's Western Adventures Productions. Released through Screen Guild the duo made six films beginning with *Dead Man's Gold*. In 1949, Lash and Fuzzy released their last film for Screen Guild, *Son of a Badman*.

The duo was off the screen for the better part of a year until Ormond made a releasing deal with Realart Pictures, the result was *The Dalton's Women* (1951). Ormond pulled out all the stops with this longer than usual (1 hr. 10 minute) opus; the supporting cast was above average, Jack Holt, Tom Neal, Raymond Hatton, Lyle Talbot, Tom Tyler, and J. Farrell MacDonald.

Although *The Dalton's Women* was a superior film in the Ormond canon, it was also at this time that he took on two powerful 'money-partners' that would go on to 'streamline' the Poverty Row budgets after this first entry. For Ormond, it may have been a necessity money-wise, for Lash and Fuzzy the end was near.

Joy Newton Houck, owner of the large chain of Joy movie theaters in Arkansas, Louisiana, and Mississippi, along with J. Francis White president of an even larger movie theater chain covering Virginia, along with North and South Carolina, decided they wanted to expand their interests by becoming motion picture producers. Forming Howco Productions (they took the initials from Houck, Ormond and White to come up with HOWCO) They contacted Ron Ormond who, along with Lash, formed a partnership to produce new films for Western Adventures and release them through Realart.

Beginning with *King of the Bullwhip*, Lash and Fuzzy were back to the under an hour grind, generally shooting their films on a five-day schedule. The film once again featured high caliber talent, Jack Holt, Tom Neal, Anne Gwynne, George J. Lewis and Dennis Moore; with this film Ron Ormond would take over as director for the final five in the series. Ironically this is the film Lash fans remember the most…probably for the movie's title more than anything else.

The final film in the series and the last of Lash and Fuzzy's films together was *The Frontier Phantom* (1952); an extremely sad end for Al St. John who would retire from film after this one, thus ending a 40-year career beginning in 1913. The 55-minute film was comprised of very little new footage used as a framing gimmick in order to use footage from the 1949 Lash and Fuzzy feature *Outlaw Country* in elongated flashbacks.

Altogether, Lash and Fuzzy made six films for the team of Houck, Ormond and White. Lash had a profit sharing agreement with Howco, but he would never see any of his collective funds from these movies. Always short of cash, Lash would borrow money against his share eventually losing his profit sharing along with any further interest funds against his contract; Lash's shares in these pictures went to Howco.

Howco (International) would eventually find its niche in releasing films to television specializing in horror, science fiction and exploitation titles like, *Brain from Planet Arous*, *Teenage Monster*, and *Ed Wood's Jail Bait*

By the early 1950s, the top western stars and characters had made their move into television; Gene, Roy, Hoppy, and the Cisco Kid where joined by The Lone Ranger. In 1953, Lash tried his hand at TV with a fifteen-minute show called *Lash of the West* on ABC. The premise was a simple one, Lash would play U.S. Marshal Lash LaRue introducing extremely truncated versions of his Ron Ormond productions. Each film would purportedly tell a story about his lookalike Grandfather also named Lash LaRue. The show lasted for 4 months; he then took to the road for personal appearances for the next 3 years.

Al LaRue as Johnny Behan in "The Life and Legend of Wyatt Earp."

Lash would not be seen on any screen again until 1956 when he showed up playing various characters on the Edgar Buchanan syndicated TV series, *Judge Roy Bean*, produced by former cowboy star Russell Hayden. He was also hired by Hayden for a one-shot appearance on his Arizona based production *26 Men* with veteran actor Tris Coffin and newcomer Kelo Henderson as the leads.

In 1960, Lash began what could have been a very good part as Sheriff Johnny Behan in *The Life and Legend of Wyatt Earp*. But trouble between Lash and *Earp* star Hugh O' Brian caused the studio to replace him with actor Steve Brodie, after 8 episodes over an eight-month period.

I did ask Hugh about their disagreement on a couple of occasions. Once when he was on a Festival of the West Q & A panel; he deflected the question by saying he didn't know anything about it. I broached the question once again at the Roy Rogers' 100th Birthday Celebration in Victorville. I found myself sitting at a luncheon table with just Hugh, fellow author Ben Costello and his son Eddie.

Ben and Eddie left for a few minutes so I decided it was time to try one more time while I had the actor all to myself.

Hugh: *I know there's been things written about a feud between the two of us, but I really don't remember there being any trouble. Lash was just being Lash on set.*

That was that. In those few words Hugh O' Brian said it all. He was now the star and "Lash" was just being "Lash." It wasn't exactly what Hugh said, but how he said it.

Lash made a few other movie and television appearances over the years, including a western porno film in 1969 called *Hard on the Trail*.

Lash: *I needed money and this guy I met offered me some to do a routine with a whip. I did the whip bit, he paid me and I left. I forgot about it, until someone asked me about my porno film. Once again, I trusted the wrong person.*

But there was nothing of real note until the television remake of *Stagecoach* (1986), starring Kris Kristofferson, Johnny Cash and Waylon Jennings.

In 1987, Waylon Jennings and Johnny Cash recorded an album called *Heroes*, dedicating it to Lash; a photo of him alongside the two singers is displayed on the back-album cover.

By 1992, when I finally interviewed Lash, he was very ill with emphysema, causing problems with his heart and blood pressure.

I can still remember Lash sitting on my right at the table used for the celebrity question and answer sessions. During the early years of the festival all the celebrities where placed together in one Q & A session; actors, stunt people, authors and musicians all at the same session. Imagine all the different questions the audience and I had for such a variety of people. Guests like: Will Hutchins (*Sugarfoot*), Irish McCalla (*Sheena, Queen of the Jungle*), Jan Merlin (*The Rough Riders*), Kelo Henderson (*26 Men*) and of course, Lash LaRue, along with several stunt people, authors and musicians all at the same table. With all these terrific people, it was kind of hard to ask a legend like Lash LaRue all the questions one would like to ask a star who was around during the heyday of the western programmers.

I didn't get a chance to 'interrogate' Lash before the program was over; so, I followed him back to his booth. He seemed tired and had been rather quiet during the Q & A. Now I realize that he probably wasn't feeling very well, but at the time I just figured that maybe he didn't want to be bothered. Still, I did have one question on my mind that I wanted to ask him.

When I got to his booth, he was sitting there, surrounded by his Lash LaRue merchandise items. With those strong, unmistakable steely, eyes he looked up at me as if to say, *"What do you want?"* Even though we had just spent the better part of an hour together, he looked at me as if it were the first time he had laid eyes on me.

I swallowed hard, stood my ground and asked my question. *"What was it like working with Fuzzy St. John?"*

His eyes soften into a wistful glance as he sat back in his chair, I truly believe for the moment he was back with his sidekick on the trail. For the first time, I saw him smile.

"Ah, Fuzzy... Fuzzy was Fuzzy." With that, he was done reminiscing.

That was it, no details, or stories, just "Fuzzy was Fuzzy." I decided to let the answer stand figuring if he wanted to add anything he would have.

I stared down at the Lash LaRue merchandise and picked one up one of the comic books, *Lash LaRue Western Annual #1*, and handed it to him. "I'd like to get this for my collection, would you sign it for me?" He signed it, *'To Charlie, Best*

Wishes. Lash LaRue. 3/21/92,' and handed it back to me. *"How much?"* I asked. He thought a moment and said, *"Go ahead and take it."*

I thanked him, said good-bye, and that was the last time I spoke to Lash LaRue.

Lash's health would continue to fade and he would stop traveling the following year. On May 21, 1995, Al "Lash" LaRue died from heart failure brought on by his long bout with emphysema.

The time I spent with Lash was very brief, less than an hour, but he did leave an impression on me. Surprisingly, although he wasn't a gregarious type like Roy Rogers or Rex Allen he didn't disappoint me. He was just like the Lash LaRue I had heard about. He was serious and not one for long explanations. He made every word count.

Those who knew him said he was suspicious of just about everyone he met in his later years; business partners had left him broke over the years and that's probably why he was staring at me so intently. I guess it was his way of figuring out if you were friend or foe.

It also may explain so many marriages; his son Ron would later tell me that no matter what the bios said about his father's number of marriages he estimated his dad to have tied the knot upwards to around 13 times. It wasn't easy, I'm sure, living up to the reputation of being Lash LaRue, but Al did it to the very end.

I still wondered what he had thought of me. He never gave me a pat on the back, a nod, or a *"Good Job"* after the interview. My answer didn't come until August of 1998, when I attended a party given by my good friends, Sharyn and Hank Sheffer. Many people from the National Festival of the West were in attendance, including Mary Brown, the festival's head honcho herself. Our conversation finally got around to Lash LaRue, and I told her how he had given me one of his comic books.

She seemed surprised. *"I think a lot of fans were turned off because he was charging for his autograph at the festival,"* (all too common at festivals these days in large part due to internet resale) *"If he gave you a book for free than he liked you! He rarely gave anybody anything for free."* I took that to be a sign. If he gave me a $2.95 comic book for free then maybe he did indeed like me after all. At least that's the way I want to think of it. Bottom line, Al "Lash" LaRue is an enigma among silver screen cowboys. He never made the top ten and yet you mention his name to any "B" cowboy fan, whether they've seen his movies or not, and they'll say, "Yeah...I've heard of him."

In 1992, on the panel I had him on, one of the questions asked by an audience member was, *"How was it working at Republic Pictures?"* Having never worked at Republic Pictures, he was a bit taken aback by the question. So little is known about the cowboy with the whip who dressed completely in black, and yet one of the things I will anxiously tell people when asked about the people I've interviewed is say, *"My first panel was with Lash LaRue."* Maybe it means something to the person I'm talking to...maybe not. But it means a whole lot to me.

CHAPTER 5
Roy Rogers

A Tale of a Tail and "Wrong Cowboy"

I admit that Roy is my idol, so if I sound too reverent towards him please forgive me. I can remember sitting in front of the television on Saturday morning, as would hundreds of other kids of all ages, and watch the

**Silver Screen Royalty
Roy & Dale**

exploits of Roy, Dale, Pat Brady, Trigger, Buttermilk, and Bullet, the Wonder Dog, as they fought the bad guys and won the day all within a half hour.

I was such a devoted fan that I named my first two dogs Bullet, even though they were Dachshunds.

Later, I discovered his movies and got hooked on them. If Roy was great on his half hour TV show he was even better in a movie!

My greatest dream was to meet Roy Rogers, but it just wasn't to be. In 1995, he was scheduled to receive the Cowboy Spirit Award, at the Festival of the West, along with Dale but due to heart surgery he was unable to attend.

However, Dale did come and it was a real pleasure to listen to her talk about her life with Roy. She even sang a song and proved that she still had what it took to entertain an audience.

I even made a special trip to Roy and Dale's museum in Victorville, California. I heard that he showed up there sometimes early in the morning to greet the crowds, but no luck. I was told that he had gone to a swap meet that morning. *"He was here just about every other morning this week,"* I was informed, which didn't make me feel any better.

To show you what a Roy Rogers fanatic I am, a few years ago Christmas fell on Wednesday, the same day Plex (the cable TV channel) has what they call Western Wednesday. For 24 hours, they show nothing but western movies (a lot of Republic

Pictures are included) and TV shows. To celebrate Christmas all they showed were Roy Rogers movies and guess who sat there for the better part of the day and night watching them? You guessed it...me! I'm just lucky that I have a family who understands my passion for Roy Rogers. So, it goes without saying that I had a great desire to meet the man.

Although I never met Roy I still have a personal story involving him that I want to share… it's a finish to a story that is mentioned in Roy and Dale's excellent book, *Happy Trails: Our Life Story*. They even talked about it during a television interview when the interviewer asked Dale if she had ever seen Roy really angry. As in the book, she told the interviewer about a trip to Oklahoma to do a show and how Trigger's tail had been completely shorn during a stopover. They had to weave a fall into Trigger's stub until his tail grew back.
"And if I ever find out who did it, I'll give 'em a piece of my mind." Roy answered.
As luck would have it, I know who the person is...and they still have a piece of the tail! It's a friend of my mother, and for a chance to meet Roy I would have gladly snitched on her.

As the friend tells the story, neither Roy nor Dale were with the crew that stopped in Prescott, Arizona, with horses used for their show, but word got out that Trigger was among them. The trouble began when, instead of watching Trigger like they were hired to do, the group went to a bar and brothel named Johnny's Place on Gurley Street, commonly known as Whiskey Row. Enter my mother's friend, who was about ten at the time, who found Trigger and snipped off a piece of the world-famous tail!

When her friends found out what she had done, she took them back to Trigger and a tail shearing frenzy ensued until nothing was left! Imagine being one of those hired hands the next morning when, amongst the haze of their hangovers, they discovered what had happened. The result was, Trigger had to be taken back to Hollywood, where a fall had to be woven into what was left of the tail.

This was the whole story which has never been told until now. It was also my ace in the hole, my entrée, to meet and talk to my idol if I was ever to get that chance.

I thought my opportunity had finally arrived a few years back when I read in the paper that Gene Autry, Pat Buttram, and Roy were coming to Phoenix for a $100 a plate dinner to honor Rex Allen to raise money for his museum in Willcox. At that time, $100 for a meal was a little too steep for my pocketbook, so going to the dinner was a little out of reach.

It was my wife, Dawn, who first mentioned the idea of calling him at the resort, where he was going to stay, and tell him the story about what happened to Trigger's tail.

"You mean, just call his room?" I laughed.

"Sure, why not?" She was determined to keep calling until she got through. Bless her for that, but I really didn't think the resort would put her in contact with Roy Rogers' room.

True to her word, on the Saturday that he was expected in town, Dawn called several times, and was told, *"Mr. Rogers hasn't arrived yet."* I figured that she was just being put off by the resort, but around 5:00 that afternoon she said that she was going to try one last time.

She called from the kitchen while I went into our bedroom. To my surprise, it wasn't long before I heard her relating the story to someone over the telephone. I ran into the kitchen to find her staring at the kitchen wall almost in a trance. I finally got her attention and mouthed to her, *"Is that Roy Rogers?"* She nodded, *"Yes!"*

Roy and Trigger

I ran into the bedroom to pick up the extension line but stopped short because I thought that it might be hard to hear over the extension. I ran back into the kitchen just in time to hear Dawn say, *"Well, I just thought you might like to know."* With that she said good-by and hung up. *"Were you really talking to Roy Rogers?"* I asked.

She nodded.

"What did he sound like?" was my next stupid question.

"Like Roy Rogers," was her reply.

My next question was, *"Why didn't you let me talk to him?"*

She finally admitted that she really didn't think she would get through and was caught off-guard. Having called the front desk, as she had been doing all day, they simply told her that *"Mr. Rogers has just gotten in,"* and put her right through. Surprised at being on the phone with Roy Rogers, Dawn forgot that the call had been made for me and told him the whole story.

Roy told her the incident happened so long ago that he wasn't mad about it anymore. With that my 'ace in the hole' evaporated; at that point in my life I had no idea what the future had in store for me and my association with the silver screen cowboys.

With that my 'ace in the hole' evaporated; at that point in my life I had no idea what the future had in store for me and my association with the silver screen cowboys.

That was several years ago. Since then I've met Roy "Dusty" Rogers, Jr., a decent performer in his own right, and Roy and Dale's daughter, Cheryl, who comes to the Festival every year and loves to talk with all the fans about her parents.

We now know there were 'Trigger' doubles, so was the one in Prescott the authentic Palomino or "Trigger Lite?" Roy would never trust a bunch of hired hands and a shared horse trailer without special supervision for Trigger; although this event happened early in Roy's career and he may not have completely owned the 'wonder horse' yet, so the question can still be raised, *"Was it the real Trigger?"*

When Roy and Dale told the story on TV and in their memoirs, they sure made it sound like the real deal and Trigger, Jr and Little Horse more than likely came later. It's all conjecture now but the time frame, early 1940's, who knows…it's still an exceptional story anyway.

Five days before I wrote this, Gene Autry passed away, just a mere three months after "The King of the Cowboys," moved on to greener pastures. Gene paved the way for Roy at Republic and Roy paved the way in Heaven for Gene, where I'm sure he met Gene with that wonderful crinkly eyed smile, saying, *"Welcome, Gene, I'm sure the good Lord'll take a likin' to ya."* I'm also sure that there's some beautiful music being made behind those pearly gates.

ADDENDUM

Since writing this chapter I've became good friends with Cheryl Rogers-Barnett and her husband Larry who both shared with me my favorite all-time silver screen cowboy story and I'd like to share it with you:

The end seemed near for Roy Rogers and his family had gathered in his hospital room. He had been in intensive care for several days and had remained unconscious for three. For cautionary purposes Roy was in an observation room, it was windowed for careful monitoring. Despite this fact, the family had closed the privacy curtain surrounding the bed.

Roy's doctor got it in his mind that he was going to lighten the mood so, upon entering the room, he pulled back the curtain and began to sing, *"I'm back in the saddle again, out where a friend is a friend."* For the first time in 3 days Roy opened one eye, lifted his head as much as he could, looked the singing doc right in his eyes and said, *"Wrong*

Cowboy." With that he laid back down and once again drifted off. Roy was eventually taken home and would pass on sometime later. That story always gets a big laugh...and to think it's true.

The two greatest singing cowboys of all time, Gene and Roy

Roy lives on in his films, in his television shows and in our hearts. He will always be there, not just a childhood memory, but a vivid memory for what he stands for. Not "stood for" but "stands for." His ideals were so strong they will forever be with those of us who rode the dusty trails of our backyards, six guns in hand, righting all wrongs.

We could do worse by our children then to introduce them to that skinny, squinty eyed silver screen cowboy who lived a morally clean life off screen as well as on. And with the condition of the world today couldn't we use him right now? The world was a little happier for having Roy Rogers and Dale Evans among us.

No, I may not have ever met my idol, but he sure did leave me with some good memories, and I can live with that. Thanks, Roy.

CHAPTER 6
John Smith

The Name's Sherman, Slim Sherman
From Dancer to Actor to Icon,
Robert Fuller
The Rita Hayworth Incident
Hell Hath No Fury Like Hathaway!

One of the common threads I found while writing this book is that a person's 'demons' can derail or destroy a successful career. Dissipation has destroyed many a performer and one of the worst is methomania or the dependence on alcohol.

Some people, like Dub Taylor, could conquer it and go on to an extremely successful career. Others, like Neville Brand, worked despite it, even though better roles could have possibly been his if not for his drinking. *"We would have to tie him to his horse, so he wouldn't fall off,"* according to *Laredo* co-star, Peter Brown.

Still others, like John Smith, had their upwardly mobile careers come to a screeching halt all from their dependence problem and, in John's case, the ire of a powerful director. Of all the people in this book, John Smith is probably the hardest for me to write about. He was a strong good looking man who had been the co-star of two NBC westerns, *Cimarron City* and *Laramie*, when he was tapped to co-star opposite John Wayne, Rita Hayworth and Claudia Cardinale in an extravagant Cinerama production, *Circus World*.

One of his most loyal fans and trusted friend, Mary Brown of Festival of the West, shared a bit of John's life, his career, and the adjustment moving forward after the debacle in Spain during the *Circus World* shoot.

For the last half of his life, John would share quite a bit about his life and career with Mary on a regular basis.

Mary: *"John got his start in* Going My Way *(1944), with Bing Crosby. He sang with the Bob Mitchell Boys Choir and if you watch it you can pick him out, because he looked the same at 14 as he did when he was 30. He was 13 or 14, I don't know. He was born March 6, 1931."*

I asked Mary about his name 'John Smith,' and life after the boys' choir?

Mary: *"His real name at that time was Robert Van Orden, Hollywood agent Henry Willson gave him the name 'John Smith.' He was working at MGM as a mimeograph operator and quickly advanced to the position of messenger. One day he was delivering scripts to the casting department and he caught the eye of casting director Jimmy Broderick. The director told him it was too bad he didn't have a SAG (Screen Actors Guild) card, because he was just the kind of kid they were looking for to play Jimmy Stewart's kid brother in* Carbine Williams (1952). *He told Broderick that he did have his card from* Going My Way, *and he got the part. He then started taking acting lessons from Lillian Burns, the acting coach at the studio, learning alongside the likes of Debbie Reynolds, Jeff Richards and Janice Rule. Unfortunately, John was taking these lessons during working hours and, when his boss found out about his extra-curricular activity, he was fired on the spot!"*

I personally interviewed John Smith for a Phoenix based TV show, *The Arizona Cowboy* in 1991. Mary was publicizing her first National Festival of the West and thought an interview with a western star like John would be just the ticket to publicize the event.

The interview was to take place at Rawhide, an old western town amusement area in Scottsdale, Arizona. Since then Rawhide has been relocated and the original site, like many other frontier locations, has fallen victim to "progress."

When he arrived, I was a bit taken aback to see "Smitty," as his friends called him. Complications from his 'physical problems' had taken their toll but he was in good spirits none the less.

My reticence went away when we sat down and talked. John was one of the nicest and most courteous men I had ever met. It was sad to think of all the wasted years of recompense for mistakes, real or otherwise, that happened almost 30 years ago.

So just how did a man who co-starred in two television series westerns, *Cimarron City* and *Laramie,* a man who John Wayne personally requested for the second lead in one of his films, end up living in a small apartment in Los Angeles and ignored by the film industry?

"Smitty" and the "Duke" from *Circus World*

Having skirted around the issue, it's now time to go back and cull what we can about what happened during 1963/1964 to cause "Smitty" to raise the ire of the director, in this case legendary filmmaker, Henry Hathaway.

The production was plagued from the start and the bad luck never seemed to let up. Frank Capra had been set to direct but left the project when John Wayne insinuated control over aspects of the production; this resulted in rewrites causing David Niven to leave the cast after agreeing to play "Cap Carson."

Rod Taylor, likewise, was set for the production playing the role of "Steve McCabe;" he too left due to the size of the role. At this point the 'legend seems to become fact.' The story goes that the Duke asked for 'John' Smith to play McCabe, but 'Roger' Smith of *77 Sunset Strip* fame was mistakenly sent for by Hathaway. If this is true it would have been a tremendous blunder to fly the wrong 'Smith' all the way to Spain just to have Wayne reject the actor, causing a waste of time and money sending him back and flying the correct 'Smith' all the way to Spain; legend number one and the first strike against "Smitty," if it were true. If it stopped there, however, Hathaway might have let it go, but his real undoing came after John Smith settled in.

"John Smith had a drinking problem for most of his adult life. His mother was an alcoholic as well." Mary went on to explain, that was a big problem in having both John and Lash LaRue as the two main attractions at the first Festival of the West. *"I think Lash and John fed off each other, alcohol wise."*

It was also around this time that he signed with talent agent Henry Willson, who changed his name from Robert Van Orden to John Smith, quite a mundane change when Willson was known for changing the names of his clients to Rock, Tab, Rory and Troy.

His first credited role was in *The High and the Mighty* (1954) with John Wayne, who became good friends with John. Based on that one movie, John Smith made the top 10 popular newcomer poll. After that he was kept busy in films like *Friendly Persuasion* (1956), with Gary Cooper.

Mary: *"You know John told me a funny story about when he was doing* Friendly Persuasion. *He and Gary Cooper were having lunch together and Cooper, who John really loved, told him that he hated to be called "Coop."*

CL: *But that's what everybody knows him by. John Wayne was "The Duke," Clark Gable or Elvis was "The King," and Gary Cooper was "Coop."*

Mary: *"Exactly, but he hated it. Anyway, he had just finished telling John how much he hated to be called "Coop," when in walked Ronald Reagan,*

slapped him on the back and said, "Hello, Coop."
John loved to tell stories about Gary Cooper."

The caliber of the stars that he worked with during this time is amazing. *Battle Circus* (1953) and *We're No Angels* (1955) with Humphrey Bogart, *Seven Angry Men* (1955) with Raymond Massey as John Brown, *Wichita* (1955) with Joel McCrea as Wyatt Earp, along with several low budget westerns with co-stars like John Derek, Nick Adams, John Payne, Kent Taylor, Tony Martin, and Chuck Connors as well as popular television programs such as, *Gunsmoke*, *Colt .45* and *Alfred Hitchcock Presents*.

In 1958 John's first attempt at a television series was a pilot called, *Sea Divers*, and then came *Cimarron City* that same year with George Montgomery and a pre-*Bonanza* Dan Blocker; the show lasted for one season.

In 1959 television stardom hit for "Smitty" when he was signed to co-star in *Laramie* with a dancer cum actor named Robert Fuller.

Ironically, *Bonanza* premiered September 12, 1959 and *Laramie* premiered September 15th, 1959, both for NBC, while *Cimarron City*'s final episode aired on NBC the following night, September 16th, 1959.

CL: *"When John was cast in* Laramie, *wasn't he originally cast in the part of "Jess" and sometime before shooting started, he and Robert Fuller changed roles."*

Mary: *"They changed parts and, I don't know how it happened, I never had the guts to ask Smitty. He was supposed to play "Jess Harper" and Bob Fuller was cast as "Slim Sherman," it's a fact.*

Robert and John had already worked together and so when Bob was approached with a western series he jumped at it. Upon reading the script he was very excited to be offered the part of "Jess Harper," feeling it was a perfect role for him; unfortunately, Revue Studios (the television division of Universal Pictures at the time) wanted him for the role of "Slim Sherman."

Robert "Bobby" Crawford the actor signed to play Slim's brother Andy fills in some information on casting:

RC: "I was already cast as Slim's brother, Andy, when they offered the role of Slim to Bob. We were both dark and slim. When he turned it down and John took it I don't think they knew how that would be accepted. It worked out great."

It does indeed make sense that, complexion and hair wise, Crawford and Robert Fuller do indeed appear more in line as brothers.

Five years after the first edition of this book went into print I began what has turned out to be a very rewarding relationship with Robert Fuller. I will let him fill in the story of the casting change from here:

RF: "Revue wanted me to play the secondary lead in a detective show called Markham *starring Ray Milland, but I want to do a western not some detective show as second banana, so I turned it down. After that, I thought I was finished and the studio would never offer me another role."* (Markham lasted one season 1958-1959 on CBS.) *"I was really surprised when they called me later to tell me they had a western they wanted me for. I read the script for* Laramie *and I got very excited about the part of Jess Harper, it was perfect for me; so, I called them as soon as I could and said I would love to play Jess."*

The studio informed him they had already offered the multi-faceted role of Jess Harper to a better-known contractee named John Smith and wanted Bob to play the less showy role of ranch-owner, Slim Sherman.

The ball was back in Bob's court and the studio was once again shocked when Robert Fuller turned down another regular show based on the character they offered.

RF: *"They couldn't believe I would turn down two different television shows, which meant steady work for an actor. I mean, who was I to turn down their offers, but I knew what I wanted and took a* chance. I firmly believed I was finished in the industry, labeled as being difficult."

Robert Fuller came to acting in a round-about way and with no forethought as to the direction his career would take; when I asked Bob if he had a game plan when it came to an acting career, he laughed and said, *"Nope."*
He further explained, *"My parents where dancers, they had a dancing school and so I learned from them."*

There it was pure and simple – which is the way Bob likes it. No big story, just that he didn't know where his ambition would take him, but he knew how to dance. And dance he did in films like, *I Love Melvin*, *Latin Lovers* and, of course, *Gentleman Prefer Blondes*, as well as appearing in non-musicals like *Above and Beyond*. He also appeared early on in one Republic Pictures western *San Antone* with Rod Cameron, Forrest Tucker, Bob Steele and Harry Carey, Jr. His roles during this time where all un-credited. It's fun to watch these films and play 'Spot Robert Fuller.'

His last film at this period in his career was the Doris Day/Howard Keel musical, *Calamity Jane.* His 'career path,' such as it was at that time, was interrupted by being drafted into the Korean War otherwise we might have only known Bob as a footnote in the waning days of Hollywood musicals or possibly as a stuntman, something he never really got out of his blood; he would turn up in full regalia in spectacles like *The Ten Commandments* and later in *Spartacus,* much to the dismay of the studio:

"After I became a known commodity I snuck on the back lot at Universal in full costume and was in the battle scenes for Spartacus *for the heck of it. When the studio found out they weren't very happy with me."*

Upon returning from Korea, Bob found himself in un-credited roles for the musicals like *Meet Me in Las Vegas* and dramas such as *The Man in the Gray Flannel Suit* with Gregory Peck as well as Humphrey Bogart's last film, *The Harder They Fall.* In 1956, he would appear uncredited in *Friendly Persuasion* in which John Smith had a featured role.

As a matter of fact, in 1956 alone Bob had seven un-credited roles under his belt; he wasn't getting any billing but that would soon change.

During this period, his best friend actor and stuntman Chuck Courtney suggested he might try his hand with acting classes to hone his skills.

Best known as Dan Reid, the Lone Ranger's nephew, on the popular TV series, Chuck would go on to a very successful career in acting, directing, producing and stunt work. He rightly received the coveted Golden Boot Award in 1994 for his body of work. These days Chuck may be known more for his turn as Billy the Kid in the cult favorite *Billy the Kid vs. Dracula*, however his career was long, varied and successful.

In 1955, it was Chuck who was the up and coming actor when Buddy Lee nee Robert Simpson, Jr. now the newly minted Robert Fuller returned from serving his country. Chuck suggested that Bob give Richard Boone's acting class a try. At this point, Boone was a couple of years from strapping on a gun as Paladin in *Have Gun Will Travel*; at the time TV viewers knew him for his episodic show *Medic* which ran from 1954 until 1956. Boone had studied at the New York Acting Studio and must have recognized Bob's talent recommending that he study with noted acting coach Sanford Meisner.

Bob continued to receive uncredited roles in such films as 1956's *Strange Intruder* with Ida Lupino, and Burt Lancaster's searing 1957 drama *Sweet Smell of Success* and would finally garner two starring roles in minor B films of 1957 that would change the direction of his career, *Teenage Thunder* with his friend Chuck Courtney (who recommended Bob for his role) and the cult horror classic, *The Brain from Planet Arous* with John Agar and Joyce Meadows

Bob's career took off with guest starring roles on TV shows like *Buckskin, General Electric Theater*, *M Squad* with Lee Marvin, *The Adventures of Rin Tin Tin, Death Valley Days, The Life and Legend of Wyatt Earp* with Hugh O' Brian, *Lawman* with John Russell and Peter Brown, *The Restless Gun* with John Payne and *Highway Patrol* with Broderick Crawford; In 1959 alone, Bob appeared in nine TV series with almost a dozen guest star appearances altogether.

It is speculated that his guest starring role on George Montgomery's *Cimarron City* in 1959 made producers take notice of Bob for series work leading to *Laramie*; John Smith who also starred in *Cimarron City* appears briefly in one scene with Bob.

The last new episode of *Cimarron City* aired on April 4th, 1959. The first episode of *Laramie* aired on September 15th of the same year. Both were on NBC. From 1959 through 1963, four seasons and 121 episodes, Slim and Jess rode together to save the day.

Incidentally, on a note of trivia, the *Laramie* theme song was originally used for the 1945 film, *Thunderhead, Son of Flicka*.

So huge was the show's fan base that during a visit to Japan in 1961, Bob was invited to have dinner with Japan's Prime Minister, Hayato Ikeda.

But did the role reversal before production began cause a rift between the two stars?

RF: *"I was very surprised when they called me back and offered the role of Jess. I don't think Smitty was happy about it, but it just worked so much better."* Mary Brown confirmed what Bob said about the change.

MB: *"Smitty wasn't very happy about the change and I'm not sure he ever got over it completely."*

"Slim" & Jess on Laramie

There's no denying that the change was the correct decision. The role of Jess required an actor that could come across as someone who had a questionable past and was now attempting a different path, while Slim was a character who constantly needed to walk the straight and arrow. The roles fit the actors to perfection.

Laramie was not an immediate success; the first three episodes did dismally. The studio then brought in veteran action film producer John Champion, younger brother of famed dancer and choreographer Gower Champion, to write and produce the program; he spiced it up and gave the characters a sound foundation.

There are also some interesting bits of trivia to go along with the 1959 western:

a. The horse that John Smith rode on *Laramie* was a chestnut gelding named "Alamo." He bought it from John Wayne, who had used the horse in his movie *The Alamo*.
b. *Cimarron City* also featured Dan Blocker who began his famed role of Hoss in 1959. *Bonanza*

premiered September 12, 1959 and *Laramie* premiered September 15, 1959, both for NBC.

c. The final *Cimarron City* episode (rerun) aired on NBC, September 16, 1959, the night following the premiere of *Laramie*.

In 1953, Revue approached Bob and Smitty about a fifth season, while Bob was agreeable John Smith turned the renewal down in favor of pursuing films.

CL: *"When the show ended in 1964, "Smitty" did* Circus World, *with John Wayne, Rita Hayworth and Claudia Cardinale."*

Mary: *"That was a big Cinerama picture filmed in Spain and directed by Henry Hathaway."*

CL: *"I was talking to Buck Taylor about directors at the last festival (1998) and he told me that Hathaway had a pretty bad temper. He said that Hathaway would kick things when he walked onto a set, and threw rocks at planes that were 30,000 feet in the air if they flew over-head and ruined a scene. I got the idea that he wasn't a pleasant guy."*

Hathaway is one of the giants of the western film genre, with movies like: *Shepherd of the Hills* (1941), *Rawhide* (1951), *How the West was Won*

(1963), *Nevada Smith* (1966), *Five Card Stud* (1968), and the film that won John Wayne his Oscar, *True Grit* (1969), among many others.

He directed his first film, *The Heritage of the Desert*, in 1932 and continued through a series of pictures based on Zane Grey novels; Grey's stipulation for a studio to retain rights to his stories was that each title had to be re-filmed every seven years. This would explain why Fox/20th Century Fox, for example, filmed *Riders of the Purple Sage* in 1918, 1925, 1931, and 1941.

Hathaway directed some of the most highly thought of and awarded films during his era including *The Lives of the Bengal Lancers* (1935) with Gary Cooper. This film alone garnered seven Oscar nominations including Best Picture and Best Director (his only nomination).

He is also credited as an innovator of 'film noir' with films like *Kiss of Death* (1947) and *Call Northside 777* (1948). He would go on to direct and produce many western favorites including: *North to Alaska* (1960), *How the West Was Won* (3 segments) (1962), *The Sons of Katie Elder* (1965),

Nevada Smith (1966), *5 Card Stud* (1968), *Shoot Out* (1971) and, of course, *True Grit* (1969).

Henry Hathaway, John Smith, Rita Hayworth, Richard Conte on the set of *Circus World*. "Smitty"'s comforting of Hayworth would cause a rift between he and Hathaway.

In a 1971 interview for the magazine *Focus on Film*, screenwriter Wendell Mayes, who worked for Hathaway on *From Hell to Texas* (1958), is quoted as saying, *"He's absolutely dreadful for actors to work with. He's probably the toughest sonofabitch in Hollywood. He is tough for a reason. Hathaway is not the most articulate man in the world, and he maintains control of his set and his crew and his actors by being cantankerous and rather cruel sometimes."*

To stress what Mayes had to say, Dennis Hopper had his budding career curtailed by Hathaway, after the young actor caused trouble on the set of *From Hell to Texas*. Hopper came from the "James Dean School of Acting," very method; Hopper had appeared in *Rebel without a Cause* with Dean and came to idolize the film's star.

His constant rebellion against Hathaway's direction on the set of the 1958 Western caused the director to tell Hopper he would never work in Hollywood again. While Hopper did continue to find independent film and television work the major offers did indeed cease.

It wouldn't be until 1965 that Hathaway finally helped lift the 'gray-listing' of the actor by casting Hopper in a small role in *The Sons of Katie Elder;* when Hopper asked the director why he decided to once again hire him, Hathaway simply said he had become a *"better and smarter actor."* In 1969

Hathaway would once again use Dennis Hopper for a small role in *True Grit*; the Academy Award winning film was released in 1969, the same year Hopper and Peter Fonda scored a huge hit with *Easy Rider*.

Hathaway's temper was very evident on the set of *Circus World* and the object of his wrath would be none other than John Smith

CL: *"So it was during the filming of* Circus World *that the incident happened many believe hurt John Smith's career?"*

Mary: *"This story was told to me by John Champion, who was a successful producer at the time this happened."* (As stated before, Champion had lead *Laramie* to success)

John Champion was indeed a very successful filmmaker. Starting as a child actor, he appeared with such greats as Leo Carrillo, Robert Young, and Charles Laughton. After the war, he turned to pulp fiction writing, and then film production, working with stars such as Rod Cameron, *Stampede* and *Panhandle* (1947-49). *Come Fill the Cup* (1951) with James Cagney. He did several with Sterling Hayden, *Hellgate*, (1952), which also starred future TV western stars James Arness and Ward Bond, *So Big* (1953), *Shotgun* (1955), *The Last Hunt* (1956) with Robert Taylor and Stewart Granger, and *Zero Hour* (1957).

Then in 1959, Champion went to work on *Laramie*, after the first few episodes failed in the ratings. He spruced it up making it one of the most fondly remembered westerns of the small screen.

He also created and produced the pilot for *McHale's Navy* (1963), and traveled to Spain to write and produce one of Audie Murphy's last films, *The Texican* (1965), which also starred Broderick Crawford. In 1975, he wrote, produced, and directed Joel McCrea in his next to last film *Mustang Country* (1975), with Robert Fuller; just for the record, McCrea's last film was an all-star salute to George Stevens called, *George Stevens: A Filmmaker's Journal* (1984). *Mustang Country* justifiably earned both the star and director National Cowboy Hall of Fame Awards.

The following story was told to Mary by John Champion, who unfortunately is no longer with us.

Mary: *"John Wayne specifically requested John Smith to play the second male lead, opposite Claudia Cardinale, who was very popular at the time. Anyway, the interesting thing that happened was that Hathaway accidentally sent for Roger Smith."*

Roger Smith had been a star in the late fifties through the early sixties in Warner's hit TV series *77 Sunset Strip*. He then appeared in a short-lived TV show based on *Mr. Roberts*. He married Ann-Margret, retiring from the limelight to manage his wife's successful career. For several years now he has suffered from Myasthenia Gravis.

Mary: *"When Roger Smith showed up in Spain, John Wayne told Hathaway that he didn't want ROGER Smith, he wanted JOHN Smith. John was in New York doing some stage work, got a call from his agent, hopped a plane and flew to Spain."*

CL: *"So they flew Roger Smith all the way to Spain, and then flew him back, and then flew John*

Smith to Spain. Is that what got Henry Hathaway mad at John Smith?"

Mary: *"That was the start, but the real incident involved Rita Hayworth. She and John stepped out drinking one night and she was supposed to be on the wagon. Hathaway got really upset about that, and he told John he was going to ruin his career and he did."*

Obviously, of the two, who is Hathaway going to blame, Rita Hayworth or John Smith? It is also believed that Hayworth was beginning to suffer from initial stages of Alzheimer's disease which may have caused some of her erratic behavior. Hayworth's odd abusive behavior and tardiness showing up on set angered John Wayne so much that he found it hard to be civil to her; he had initially been excited to work with her.

The Duke had already faced a set-back on the set when he had wanted Rod Taylor for the part of Steve McCabe, the Australian actor pulled out just before filming due to the size of the role. Wayne once again asked for Taylor on the film *The War Wagon* in 1967, the studio wanted a bigger name hiring Kirk Douglas; Duke and Taylor would eventually appear together in the rather dismal film *The Train Robbers* in 1973.

Circus World - The scene that almost ended John Wayne's career

Then there was the fire that would hasten the Duke's health problems. The fire, an integral part of the film, got out of control trapping Wayne inside a burning tent. Obviously, Duke made it out as the tent fell around him but the smoke inhalation he experienced accelerated what turned out to be early-stages of lung cancer.

Not getting Rod Taylor, the burning tent incident, Hathaway sending for the wrong 'Smith,' and Rita Hayworth's erratic behavior all added up to someone becoming a fall-guy for all the bad-luck...that turned out to be none-other than "Smitty."

In the photos, I have included of John Smith, it's obvious how uneasy he is with Hathaway trying to show him how to dance and kiss Claudia Cardinale. In the kissing scene John is trying to pull away from Hathaway. Whether the famous director was trying to purposely embarrass John Smith is not known. You can be the judge whether Hathaway was trying to make "Smitty" uneasy or not, his hands-on approach gives an example of how exact the director was in displaying what he wanted his actors to get across on screen.

CL: *"Hathaway told him right to his face that he would ruin his career?"*

Mary: *"Well, that's what John Champion told me. He told him that he would never work in Hollywood again, and he basically didn't."*

CL: *"So, moving forward, from about 1965 on, his career was basically over?"*

Mary: *"Just some very, very small television parts, but really nothing."*

Looking at John's IMDb page of appearances after *Circus World* one would assume he would go on to larger roles...this was not the case. There would be 16 appearances by John Smith between 1964 and his retirement in 1978, mostly guest spots on TV shows and one western film *Waco* in 1966 in support of Howard Keel, Jane Russell and Brian Donlevy for R.G. Springsteen.

CL: *"So all the problems around the set were compounded by Smitty's going out on the town with Rita Hayworth?"*

Mary: *"That's what I was told by John Champion. They fed off each other with their drinking problems.*

Rita Hayworth's last film *The Happy Thieves* in 1961 had been a flop; her last real hit had been in 1959 with Gary Cooper in *They Came to Cordura*. She had been working hard for her comeback with *Circus World* and to prepare for it she had gone totally 'on the wagon,' so to speak. Unfortunately, the combination of Rita Hayworth and John Smith working so closely in Spain made for a combustible situation.

Aggravating her already fragile mood the night out caused things to worsen…and the blame for all of it fell on John.

CL: *"So, here's this successful actor who had a nice house on Mullholland Drive and he lost it all?"*

Mary: *"He ended up living in the bungalow of a house his mother owned down by La Brea and I-10. Not a very good section.*

You know, Laramie *could have gone on another year, but John left the show. He didn't want to do another year but he had a five-year contract and had only done four. So, they had to put him in something else or pay him off. They paid him off, and Bob Fuller went right into* Wagon Train *and then* Emergency.

Robert Fuller joined *Wagon Train* in 1962, as Cooper Smith after a one season interim after Robert Horton's departure. Denny "Scott" Miller remained as the lone scout during that season. Denny was already an established actor when the producers of the program decided he needed to change his name. As Denny explained:

Denny: *"I had already done quite a bit including a stint in a Tarzan movie for MGM when they were toying with the idea of bringing it back to its original studio. The* Wagon Train *producers insisted on changing my first name to "Scott" because they felt "Denny" wasn't manly enough. They said, 'any man's name that ends with 'ie' or 'y' a hard 'e' sound isn't manly. I'll bet Johnny Mack Brown or Johnny Weissmuller would have disagreed."*

L*aramie* left the air on September 17, 1963. Another interesting sidebar is that John Smith auditioned for the part of "Flint McCullough," the part that went to Robert Horton, making him a star.

Luana Patten and John at their wedding

On June 4, 1960, John married actress Luana Patten (*Song of the South, Home from the Hill, Go Naked in the World*). In her column of Sunday, June 26, 1960, powerful gossip columnist Hedda Hopper ran a piece on John and Luana, one of the quotes from John went as thus: *"The house is on Mulholland, Dan Duryea is one of our neighbors. We have about an acre, a wonderful view, four bedrooms and three baths."*

In her comments, Hopper went on to add, "When I suggested they must be expecting a large family, they both laughed and said in the same breath, "We'll try to be good Catholics."

CL: "Now, when I was getting ready to do the interview with him, in '91, you told me not to be shocked by his appearance..."

Mary: "...and you were."

CL: "And I was. You could tell it was him, but he was in bad shape."

Mary: "Yeah, he was."

CL: "He had been convalescing for a few days, just for the interview."

Mary: "Yeah, he rallied just to come over, which was a very major thing for him."

CL: *"And then, he wasn't sure he was going to show up for the festival."*

Mary: *"We never knew when he was going to show up."*

CL: *"But he did show up for the first festival."*

Mary: *"That's right."*

CL: *"I think the festival made him nervous, and he needed support.*

Mary: *"I'd go to his house sometimes and I'd never know which John I was going to find. You know, I can watch episodes of* Laramie *and I can tell you which ones he's sober in and I can tell you which ones he's not sober in.*

CL: *"There's a distinct difference?"*

Mary: *"Oh! A very distinct difference. As a matter of fact, I was just down at the Western Music Association and I was talking with Johnny Western, and he said that he had just had a very lengthy conversation with Bob Fuller about John Smith. Bob was saying that it was so sad, because he had tried to help John, but he just couldn't do anything for him."*

Robert Fuller was indeed instrumental in getting "Smitty" the role of Captain Hammer in back to back episodes on the first season of *Emergency* (1972).

At this point, Mary asked if I would like to see her John Smith Memorabilia. Does a chicken have lips? I sure did! We went upstairs to her festival office where she showed me her extensive collection of John Smith pictures and memorabilia, some of it one of a kind items that John had given her.

It was fascinating and put everything into perspective. John Smith may have been his own worst enemy, but he left his fans a body of work that we can watch and enjoy again and again.

I knew that Mary was an avid John Smith fan and had been since she was a kid. John and Mary visited often, on the phone and in person, but I was curious as to why he took such a liking to her. I think Mary's *"It's because Mary cared enough to remember him."*

ADDENDUM

Because of *Laramie,* Robert Fuller and John Smith will be forever linked with western fans. The show continues to draw enthusiasts from around the world to western festivals. While Bob continues to draw huge crowds wherever he goes, there are plenty of stories about "Smitty."

Robert Fuller will always pay tribute to John and the stories he shares are always told in the best of fun and very honorable to John's memory. Like any special friend, I've found Bob to never say anything that would lessen the memory of "Smitty," and I respect that immensely.

I won't go into the many stories about the "trouble" these two caused – with help from a cast of characters that included Frank McGrath and Terry Wilson from *Wagon Train.* Needless-to-say they would pay a few visits to Universal Pictures president Lew Wasserman's office from time to time to do penance. It all makes for some great festival stories for sure, to be told at a different time.

The one thing to remember is that while they made an effective team on *Laramie* they should be honored for the contributions they made separately to the western genre and continue to make through the memories of those who know Robert Fuller and those who knew John Smith.

CHAPTER 7
Buck Taylor

*The Legend Lives On
From Cannonball to Newly
Chauffeur to Water Colors*

One of the wonderful things about the Festival of the West is that you get to meet and become friends with people you thought you'd never have that chance to talk with. One of these is Buck Taylor.

From 1967 through 1975, we watched Buck as Newly O' Brien on *Gunsmoke*. Before that he appeared in such television shows such as: *Wagon

Train (1957), *Combat* (1962), *The Big Valley* and *The F.B.I.* (1965) as wel as a featured player on *The Monroes* (1966) as John "Brad" Bradford. His early movie roles include: *And Now Miguel* and *The Wild Angels* (1966) and *The Devil's Angels* and *The St. Valentine's Day Massacre* (1967).

Since his days as Newly he has appeared in numerous television shows and motion pictures such as: *The Sacketts* (1979), *The Legend of the Lone Ranger* (1981), *Triumphs of a Man Called Horse* (1982), *The Alamo: Thirteen Days to Glory* (1987) *Conagher* (1991), *Gettysburg* (1993), *Tombstone* (1993) and *Rough Riders* (1997), as well as a return to Newly O' Brien in *Gunsmoke: Return to Dodge* in 1987.

Recently Buck costarred with Burt Reynolds in the film *Hard Time*, in which Burt returned to the type of hard edged role that made him the number one box office star for five consecutive years from 1978-82

Buck was born to the acting world growing up around his father, the very popular character actor, Dub Taylor, and his Hollywood friends.

Bob Wills, Russell "Lucky" Hayden & Dub "Cannonball" Taylor

Dub's lengthy career started on an extremely high note appearing in *You Can't Take It with You* (1938) for Frank Capra; he won the role of Ed Carmichael due to the fact he could play the xylophone with such expertise.

Columbia, however, saw fit to place Dub as a "B" western sidekick rather than another "A" film; Capra did use him as an unbilled reporter in *Mr. Smith Goes to Washington* in 1939.

His sidekick moniker "Cannonball" would carry him through numerous 'Oaters' at Columbia and Monogram, with a stopover for one film at Republic Pictures with Don "Red" Barry – unable to use the Columbia Picture's name of "Cannonball" at Republic he was called "Nevady" for the film, *One Man's Law* (1940); Columbia would briefly replace him as "Cannonball" with actor/comic Frank Mitchell for seven films in 1941 and 1942.

"I grew up close to the old Republic Studio and used to sneak in and play on the lot." Buck would tell me. *"My dad made over 500 pictures. I grew up in the San Fernando Valley where we had a little adobe house. Our neighbors were Yakima Canutt, Roy Rogers lived further out in Encino, Monte Hale lived near us. I lived near Republic Studios, which was a couple of river bottoms from my place. I look back at the environment I grew up in and it was thrilling. Chill Wills was my dad's best friend and Guinn "Big Boy" Williams lived down the road and Russell Hayden.*

I grew up with cowboys that came from all over the United States to get in the movies. I grew up with Joe and Cap Canutt, who became Charlton Heston's stuntman. I never paid much attention to all this, because I figured that's the way most kids grew up." (Before the studio became Republic Pictures, it was Mack Sennett's studio and is now owned by CBS.)

Many people believe that Dub finished his days as "Cannonball" at Monogram with Jimmy Wakley in 1949, but that isn't quite correct. His last time using the name and pulling sidekick duties was for 1950 TV pilot starring none other than Wild Bill Elliott called *The Marshal of Trail City.*

After Dub finished out his sidekick duties, he jumped into television with *Casey Jones* (1958) as Wallie Sims for 78 episodes alongside Alan Hale, Jr. as Casey. But it was Dub's long career as an on-screen character actor in such films as: *No Time for Sergeants* and *Auntie Mame* (1958), *A Hole in the Head* (1959), *Sweet Bird of Youth* (1962), *Spencer's Mountain* (1963), *The Hallelujah Trail, Cincinnati Kid* and *Major Dundee* (1965), *Bonnie and Clyde* (1967), *Three for Texas* and *Bandolero!* (1968), *The Reivers, Death of a Gunfighter, The Wild Bunch* and *The Undefeated* (1969), *A Man Called Horse*

(1970), *Support Your Local Gunfighter* (1971), *The Getaway* (1972), *Pat Garrett and Billy the Kid* (1973), *Cannonball Run II* (1984), *Back to the Future III* (1990), *Conagher* (1991), *The Gambler Returns* (1991) and *Maverick* (1994), to name a sampling that got him attention. His episodic TV appearances are just as impressive, *The Roy Rogers Show*, *Dragnet, I Love Lucy, Cheyenne, Lawman, Laramie, The Life and Legend of Wyatt Earp, Perry Mason, Burke's* Law, *The Virginian, Laredo, The Man from Uncle, The* Monkees, *Bonanza,* the list goes on and on. Dub also gained notoriety from his many guest appearances on *The Tonight Show* with Johnny Carson and his *Hubba Bubba Bubble Gum* and *Pace Picante Sauce* commercials.

One of my most prized possessions hanging on the wall of our family room is a print of Buck's most popular watercolor called, "My Dad and Me." Inscribed on it is a message from Buck that says: "Dear Charlie, Our Dads our Special." I treasure the work and the thought. The following are excerpts from Q & A sessions with Buck separately and with other celebrities:

CL: *"Let's start with your father, way back before there was a Buck Taylor. How did he get the name Dub?"*

Buck: *"His name was Walter Clarence Taylor, Jr., and down in the south they call you W.C., then W. and then "Dub". So, it ended up Dub."*

CL: *"He was a performer, went to New York and that's where he met your mother."*

Buck: *"My dad was born in Richmond, Virginia in 1907, but he attended high school in Oklahoma City and from there he entered Vaudeville. He played two instruments the harmonica and the xylophone, and he was one of the best in the world at both-of-them."* He toured and would run into Will Rodgers and Al Jolson.

My mother and her sister were dancers and did an act together. My dad saw a photograph of her and her sister and he said, 'I'm gonna marry that woman,' and he did."
They toured together until my sister was born and then my mother retired. Vaudeville was slipping away, due to movies talking at that point and taking over, and my dad was losing a job there.

That was in 1937 and Frank Capra was doing a movie with James Stewart and Jean Arthur called, You Can't Take It with You, *a huge movie that garnered a lot of Academy Awards (Best Picture and Director). Capra needed a Xylophone player. Frank Capra interviewed my dad and he got the part, in fact, while he was out in Hollywood I was born during the trip* (May 13). *I was born in a building at Hollywood and Western Boulevard, so I guess you could say that I was born to play in Hollywood Westerns."*

In his autobiography, The Name Above the Title, Frank Capra recalls that Dub played the song *Dinah* at his audition:

Capra: *"I was interviewing xylophone players when in walked a merry oaf wearing a perpetual infectious grin as big as a sunburst. Sweat drops gleamed on his receding forehead. 'I'm Dub Taylor, suh, and I kin play the xylophone.' His very presence evoked laughter. 'Have you ever played in a picture, Mr. Taylor?' I asked. 'No suh, I ain't.'*

Dub and Ann Miller in You Can't Take It with You. Both would go on to very successful careers

Capra went on to say that Dub made *Dinah* sound like "four anvil choruses," which must have impressed the Academy Award winning director because he "cast him on the spot."

Buck: *"He got the part, and went under contract to Columbia studios after that, and went on to play in 'B' westerns portraying a guy named Cannonball."*

CL: *"He went from acting in a Frank Capra film to becoming a sidekick at Columbia for 'Wild Bill' Elliott."*

Gordon Elliott was a supporting player, usually on the wrong side of the law in gangster films, until he was cast against type as the lead in the Columbia serial, *The Great Adventures of Wild Bill Hickok*. From there he became known as Bill or William, depending on the budget of the picture. He was the only western star under contract to Republic Pictures, besides John Wayne, to go from programmer westerns to 'A' westerns at the studio.

Starting at Columbia as Wild Bill Hickok, the character would trade last names back and forth going from Hickok to Saunders to Elliott. Dub eventually joined Elliott, as a character known as "Cannonball."

When asked why Dub was called "Cannonball," Charles Starrett one of Dub's later co-stars put it succinctly, *"He looked like a Cannonball."*

As mentioned earlier, after Dub left the "Wild Bill" series his moniker of "Cannonball" was given to a much thinner comic by the name of Frank

Mitchell, who replaced him in the Elliott programmers. Later, Dub would reclaim his "Cannonball" character and take it with him for his Monogram series with Jimmy Wakely.

"Wild Bill" Elliott

As mentioned earlier, after Dub left the "Wild Bill" series his moniker of "Cannonball" was given to a leaner comic by the name of Frank Mitchell, who replaced him in the Elliott programmers. Later, Dub would reclaim his "Cannonball" character and take it with him for the Jimmy Wakely series at Monogram.

Through the 1940's, Dub would be the sidekick to Elliott, Tex Ritter, Russell Hayden, and Charles Starrett at Columbia, Don "Red" Barry at Republic, and Jimmy Wakely at Monogram.

Buck: *"His favorite actor to work with was Russell Hayden, because they had a lot of fun together. Bill Elliott was great, too, but Russell and he had a lot of fun.*

Russell "Lucky" Hayden went on to produce several western TV shows

You know, Roy Rogers had The Sons of the Pioneers, "Lucky" Hayden and my dad had Bob Wills and the Texas Playboys, which was a neat band. If you see any of those old films, Bob Wills does a song like every ten minutes. They're all like little music videos of songs you'll never hear again, and it's really unique."

CL: *"When your father left the Charles Starrett "Durango Kid" westerns at Columbia, Starrett was quoted as saying that he was very upset when* your *dad left because he enjoyed working with him and wished that he continued in the series. That's a pretty big compliment, when you think that it was Smiley Burnette who took his place."*

Columbia signed Burnette to a contract after he left Republic Pictures. At Republic Smiley had been as popular as many of the silver screen cowboys he did sidekick duty with, but once Gene Autry left for active duty during World War II Republic concentrated on George "Gabby" Hayes whose contract stipulated he would appear in both "A" and "B" films.

Smiley left the studio after *Firebrands of Arizona* with Sunset Carson in 1944. In 1946, Columbia signed Burnette to appear in the Durango Kid series with Charles Starrett, much to Starrett's displeasure; this meant that Dub was out in favor of Smiley Burnette's name-value.

The former Republic Picture's mainstay didn't make it any easier for Starrett to accept the change when he took it upon himself to informed the star that he had been signed by the studio to help the "sagging popularity" of the Durango Kid series.

Dub's last western series film for Columbia, *Frontier Gunlaw* was released in January of 1946. It wouldn't be until October 1947 that Dub returned to sidekick duties alongside Jimmy Wakely at the much lower budget studio, Monogram. Unlike Burnette who was forced to surrender his "Frog Millhouse" character name upon leaving Republic Pictures, Columbia had no more use for the sidekick name, "Cannonball;" by this time Dub was so identified by the name that it would have been superfluous for Columbia to give it to any other sidekick.

Wakley's reaction to his new sidekick was just the opposite of Starrett's for ole' Dub. Wakley was quoted as saying that he felt Dub's humor was "too broad" for his films; it's interesting to note that neither Starrett nor Wakley were happy with the change.

CL: *"When your father left the Charles Starrett "Durango Kid" westerns at Columbia, Starrett was always quoted as saying that he was very upset when your dad left because he enjoyed working with him and wished that he continued in the series. How did he* (Dub) *feel about the move to a lower echelon Poverty Row Studio like Monogram?"*

Buck: *"I think as an actor you don't have a choice. I mean things change, different people come into power, they're in, you're out. I don't think my dad was real happy at Monogram with Jimmy Wakely. I don't know if they really got along that well. I don't like to say anything bad, but that really wasn't one of his favorites to work with after riding with Elliott, Ritter, Hayden, Starrett and Barry."*

The Wakely series also had the dubious distinction of introducing Whip Wilson, before he moved on to his own western series, albeit with some great sidekicks like Andy Clyde and Fuzzy Knight.

Buck: *"Dad had a spell where he wasn't hired for a long time. He drank quite a bit, like everyone else did in those days. and things got a little rough for him, I remember. Then he quit drinking and got his way back into Hollywood, because the rumor got around that he quit drinking and that he was trying to help himself. That's when he started landing* *some really good movie parts in big films. Frank Capra hired him again in a movie (*A Hole in the Head) *and then his movie career just escalated from* Bonnie and Clyde *until he passed away."*

CL: "I

Jimmy Wakely enjoying a little sax with Dub "Cannonball" Taylor

understand that for a long time your dad didn't even want to talk about his career as a sidekick."

Buck: *"I don't think he was ashamed, or anything like that, it's just that my dad didn't like to live in the past. What has happened, happened, and I don't think he liked to reminisce."*

CL: *"Did he mind being called Cannonball, as some reports say?"*

Buck: *"He didn't mind that. I mean, it's like me being called Newly, I'll be called that the rest of my life. I called him 'Cannonball' and so did his grandkids. My career parallels my dad's, in a way. I started out doing a popular western series, with a certain amount of popularity, which I realize now is immortal. Then your career kind of slides off a little bit, and then I quit drinking ten years ago and people started hiring me; like in the case of* Tombstone. *I asked Kevin Jarre, 'Now, why did you decide you wanted me in this movie?' and he said, 'Cause I watched* Gunsmoke *growing up as a kid every Saturday night in Wyoming.'*

Things make a circle and they come around. It's interesting, the people that hire me now in Hollywood are in their late 30s or early 40s and they were fans from Gunsmoke.*"*

CL: *"Speaking of* Gunsmoke, *you appeared on the show before you became a regular. Your character's name was Leonard Parker and you got shot!"*

Buck: *"I was John Ireland's son and James Stacy shot me. I thought I was the fastest gun in the west, but I was wrong."*

(This was a two-part episode *Vengeance* which aired October 9, 1967.)

"I figured, 'that's it for Gunsmoke,' and it wasn't a month later that I tested for the part of Newly. Actually, they wanted Michael Anderson (The Monroes) for the part but he turned it down. When I tested for the part his name was Newly Jorgensen (pronounced "Yorgensen"). They tested five guys and I got the part and they said, 'You're not Jorgensen, you're O'Brien,' because I'm Irish.

You know, my dad schooled me in the way to deal with people, and then Milburn Stone and Ken Curtis put the finishing touches to me, because they were the masters at dealing with the public. They told me that if you go to a rodeo, you sit down and sign autographs until the very last little kid leaves.

Doc (Milburn Stone) *told me, 'You're going to be accepted in a family, because this show is like a family, and people will come up and they'll hug you, they'll know you.' And that's the way people receive me to this day."*

Gunsmoke debuted in 1955 and finished its original run in 1975. Along the way, Dennis Weaver became a star when he appeared as Chester Goode, Burt Reynolds was a regular playing blacksmith Quint Asper, and a former singing cowboy, Son of the Pioneers member, and big band singer, Ken Curtis became famous as a lovable codger named Festus – here legend raises its ugly head again and tells us that Ken replaced Frank Sinatra with Tommy Dorsey's band on a regular basis, but even Curtis himself dispelled that as non-factual.

The following is a portion of a Q & A session where Buck was joined by Harry Carey, Jr. and Johnny Western.

CL: "Gunsmoke *expanded to an hour in 1961, at that time, there were up to 30 westerns on network TV each week.*"

Johnny: "*Bob Hope used to joke back then that NBC meant 'Nothing But Cowboys.'*"

CL: "Gunsmoke *was actually cancelled in 1967 and isn't it true that because William Paley, the*

President of CBS at the time, was a Gunsmoke *fan it was reinstated?"*

Buck: *"I think it was that, and the fact that it was doing well in the ratings. The people who buy the shows, the affiliates, were going to drop shows if they didn't put* Gunsmoke *back on. They were getting so much feedback from the people who watched the show, so, along with Paley having faith in the show, it stayed on."*

The full story behind *Gunsmoke* being re-instated had more to do with Paley's wife Barbara 'Babe' Paley being a major fan of the show and insisting it be placed back on the schedule; its cancellation was even discussed on the floor of the U.S. Congress at the time. To make re-instatement possible CBS needed to find 30 minutes in the schedule to air the second half of the program; as a result, *Gilligan's Island* was dropped for what would have been its 4th season.

CL: *"I understand that the cast had even had their rap party for the show."*

Buck: *"Yeah, I wasn't on at that time. I came on the next year.*

The reason a popular show like *Gunsmoke* could be cancelled was because networks started to rely on a thing called "demographics" in the late 60s; this period is commonly known as the "Rural Purge." Still popular shows were taken off the air due to their audience age and location.

Simply put, demographics were a way of networks finding out what types and age groups were watching their shows, then go for what they consider their future base.

If a show was getting a high rating, but the group was deemed unappealing to the network and sponsors i.e. to an older audience (*Ed Sullivan* or *Red Skelton*), or if a show was too rural (*Beverly Hillbillies* or *Green Acres*), the networks and sponsors felt that the buying power wasn't as strong as say those watching urban adventures like the original *Hawaii 5-O*, *The Prisoner*, or *The Mod Squad* or pablum like *Here Come the Brides*, *The Flying Nun* and *Land of the Giants*. Thus, many good and high rated shows were cancelled before their popularity diminished.

Marshal Matt Dillon (James Arness), "Doc" Adams (Milburn Stone),
Miss Kitty Russell (Amanda Blake), Quint Asper (Burt Reynolds) & Festus Haggen (Ken Curtis).

CL: "Gunsmoke *was so popular that it was mentioned in Congress when it was being cancelled, but do you know that to reinstate the show CBS had to cancel a half hour comedy, so they could give* Gunsmoke *its full hour?"*

Buck: *"I didn't know that."*

CL: *"They had to cancel* Gilligan's Island.*"*

Dobe: *"I did about twelve or thirteen* Gunsmokes.*"*

CL: *"Buck, how about your dad? How many did he do?*

Buck: *"Three or four, but I was never in one with him."* (For the record, Dub did 7 episodes from 1966 – 1970).

CL: *"It's interesting when you hear all the various actors who tested for the part of Marshal Dillon. Raymond Burr, Denver Pyle and the radio voice of Matt Dillon, William Conrad, the radio show's Marshal Dillon. He found lasting fame as* Cannon. *That would have been a different kind of Dillon."*

Buck: *"You know, I saw a movie on TV with William Conrad and Anthony Quinn, where he (Conrad) was the lawman and it was terrific. He didn't look like the kind of sheriff that we think of, but he was fantastic. It was a good movie."*

CL: "*That's* The *Ride Back (1957).* I know that it's a common belief that John Wayne was asked to play Marshal Dillon, which we know to be one of those Hollywood myths, but he did recommend an actor he had under contract for the part."

Buck: "*That's true, and the actor was James Arness.*"

CL: "*Denver Pyle told me last year that he had the role pretty much sewed up. The producers told him they had just one more actor to look at, but not to worry because they thought the other actor would be too tall.*"

Buck: "*Jim Arness was under contract to John Wayne's production company, Batjac, and John Wayne loved him. I remember seeing this TV show where John Wayne was presenting an award to Jim. Duke was standing out there on stage next to the microphone and Jim Arness walks out. Duke hands him this award, looks at him, and says, 'You're bigger than me.' And James Arness says, 'Taller maybe.' I'll never forget that.*

As you got to know Jim, he was a very funny guy. I'd have a hard time looking him in the eye when I was acting with him. I couldn't keep a straight face."

CL: *"John Wayne introduced the first episode"*
Buck: *"He did."*

CL: *"Who were some of the future stars that appeared on* Gunsmoke?*"*

Buck: *"I did one with Richard Dreyfuss and I don't even remember doing it. Jon Voight, who was just on the brink of being successful; he just did the film,* Midnight Cowboy, *but it hadn't been released yet. People were talking about it and sure enough, he became a big star. You know Gary Busey did the last* Gunsmoke.*"*

"I also did an episode of Simon and Simon, *and I went up to those two guys (Gerald McRaney & Jameson Parker) to introduce myself, you know nobody was more popular at the time then those two. Anyway, one of them said, 'Buck, we know you, we've both been on Gunsmoke!' Harrison Ford also did one."*

CL: *"How is James Arness doing?"*

Buck: *"I'm not sure. He had a bad leg all through* Gunsmoke. *He was wounded on Salerno*

Beach in Italy during World War II, and he always had a lot of pain in it. I think that's giving him a lot of problems. I haven't spoken to him in about 10 years, but I'd like to call him and tell him just how loved he is by a lot of people. I'd also like to paint a portrait of him." (James Arness passed away on June 3rd, 2011, but not before Buck did a few watercolors of him).

Denver Pyle and Charlie

CL: *"How is James Arness doing?"*

Buck: *"I'm not sure. He had a bad leg all through Gunsmoke. He was wounded on Salerno Beach in Italy during World War II, and he always had a lot of pain in it. I think that's giving him a lot of problems. I haven't spoken to him in about 10 years, but I'd like to call him and tell him just how loved he is by a lot of people. I'd also like to paint a portrait of him."* (James Arness passed away on June 3rd, 2011, but not before Buck did a few watercolors of him).

Johnny: *"Buck, my favorite story about your dad involves the xylophone. Tex Ritter was a favorite of a lot of people in Texas and had a great roadshow. He would take comedians on the road with him for years and he took your dad out on the road with him.*

They were playing in Houston or San Antonio, Texas for some big deal at a very swanky place. People were paying a ton of money to be there and Tex was playing the straight man to Dub and then, to everybody's amazement, he put your dad over on the xylophone. He was wonderful, and this very wealthy multi-millionaire Texan started sending hundred dollar bills up on the stage to have your dad play the same song over and over and over. Every time Tex would try to get back to the show, this guy would send another hundred dollar bill up to get Dub to play this song again.

Anyway, it ended up that the guy sent about $1,200 up on stage and as long as he kept sending the hundreds Tex couldn't sing because Dub kept playing.

Tex Ritter

So finally, Tex just snorted into the microphone and said, 'Cannonball, the show must go on. Maybe you could entertain this gentleman in your room later on with the xylophone.' To make a long story short, the guy had the xylophone carried up to Dub's room, in the same hotel where they were playing, and Dub played about three more tunes and the guy gave him $1,500 and the guy bought the xylophone from him before the night was over."

Buck: "That's a true story. The guy's name was Buck York and he was from Midland, Texas. This was like in the 40's or 50's and he would fly my dad to Midland, have him play for the night at a party he was giving. The song was Melancholy Rose that he liked him to play, and he'd play the same song all night.

Buck York had another ranch in Las Vegas, New Mexico and he said to my dad, "I got the ticket for you, it'll take you to Albuquerque and then take a taxi." It's like 150 miles to his ranch, so my dad got in a taxi and it took him all the way out there. To this guy, money was no object, he was a wealthy oilman, but he would import my dad to play the same song all the time."

Johnny: *That night, on the Tex Ritter show, your dad made more money than Tex did."*

Dobe: *"The last time I worked with Dub, he was one of the dearest gentleman that ever lived, and I worked with him on* Back to the Future III. *He, Pat Buttram and I just sat at this card table and had a couple of lines, but they paid us good to do that.*

We're sitting there on the set, up in Sonora, and I wasn't as deaf as I am now, but Dub was deafer. So, Dub said, in that funny Georgia accent, 'Ah kin't Heah.' (Translation: I can't hear).

So, I said, 'When they say 'action', I'll kick you under the table.' He said, 'Good.' Now Dub has been in more movies than I have, but he's sitting there and the guy with the clapper yells, "Action!" and Dub says, 'Wha'd he say?' And we had to start all over again."

Buck: *"When he got older, he did a scene with a guy and he said; 'Now lissen, I'll staht talkin' when you stop.' So, he would actually look at this guy and it was great, because he was really looking at him like he was listening to him, and when he'd stop talking my dad would say his lines."*

CL: *"Buck, you were inducted into the Cowboy Hall of Fame in 1981, so you're not a stranger to awards. I believe your award is the Trustee Award, what exactly is that?"*

Buck: *"The entire show (Gunsmoke) was put into the Hall of Fame. I was awarded the Trustee Award, along with Glenn Strange, whereas James Arness, Amanda Blake and Ken Curtis had a portrait painted of them and put it in there. With me, it's just my name.*

My goal, and this is something I haven't told a lot of people, since I'm in the Cowboy Hall of Fame as an actor, I think it would be a real nice goal for me to try to get in there as an artist. To have a piece of my work in there, that would really thrill me."

In 2006, Buck was awarded his own Western Heritage Award in recognition for his work; he also has a plaque on the Walk of Western Stars in Santa Clarita, California, that includes past recipients James Arness and other *Gunsmoke* alumni Dennis Weaver and Amanda Blake.

One thing we haven't really talked about is Buck's immense talent at painting with watercolors.

Buck: *"I wanted to be an artist as a little boy. My father had some Russell prints and I would admire how Russell had captured the cowboy life of our* past. That interested me and then to be able to perform in cowboy movies and paint from my experiences, it's really a nice thing.

I majored in art all through school and I attended Chouinard Art Institute of Los Angeles, while I was in high school, but I received a gymnastics scholarship to USC, Penn State, and the Air Force Academy. I chose to go to USC, but I failed my math class and they took my scholarship away and gave it to a Hungarian refugee. So that let me out of school and the navy activated me.

I stayed in the navy for two years, got out, and the first thing that happened was a stuntman named Ronnie Rondell said that there was a gymnastics stunt that I should do, and I did.

So, I did some stunt work, and then some acting parts and I just gave up the painting. I didn't paint much for 30 years."

CL: "What happened to make you start painting again?"

Buck: "About ten years ago, I wasn't working much and I owed a lot of money. A lot of people don't know this, but, at night I was driving a limousine for five bucks an hour and tips. People would recognize me and say, 'Aren't you a movie star?' or 'Weren't you Newly?' Things like that, and I'd say 'No.' I was approaching 50 and I got to thinking that there had to be something else I could do. I felt I had started at the top and I was working my way down.

So, I started my brain to working and this voice kept saying, 'You studied art.' But I thought, 'Yeah, but there were thousands of artists out there.'

I made this statement to this lady I knew, 'You know, I think I'm going to get back into my artwork,' and she said, 'Oh, that's great.' I knew I couldn't face her again if I didn't have something. I started sketching, started painting. I went to a life drawing workshop and I could see the improvement in my painting and then it was like a passion. I just really got into it. The first year I made more money than I ever did driving limousine.

I got in galleries, things like that, and then I pulled out of the galleries after I started the festivals like this."

CL: "I remember when you first started here eight years ago. Things have sure changed since then."

Buck: "*I didn't know what I was doing. I had artwork hanging from the bleachers. (A major portion of the festival was held in a pavilion behind the rodeo bleachers at Rawhide.) At the end of two or three days, another artist, Carlos Hadaway, came up to me and said, 'Do you have any idea of your potential?' I said, 'No.' He said, 'Well, you sold all of your little paintings,' and I said, 'I know.' He asked me if I was serious about wanting to do this and I told him I was.*

He told me to get out a piece of paper and I wrote everything he told me. He said, 'Think of it! You've been on Gunsmoke, *somewhere in the world once a week since 1967!' It's a fact and it's really helped me with my artwork.*

You know painting is similar to acting. You create something on paper or canvas and with acting you create a character on film. The difference is, it's nice when someone says they enjoyed you on Gunsmoke, *but to go into someone's home and see a painting of yours hanging over their fireplace, that's a great feeling. I'll look at it and I'll remember when I painted it. It's a real nice thing. It's bought me a ranch and got me out of debt, changed my entire life.*

I painted a lot from Tombstone, *which Dobe and I were in together. And since then* The Roughriders, Gettysburg, *and all these different films that I make, it's a real blessing and I'm grateful to do it, because now I can work as much as I want, or as little as I want."*

CL: *"You have four children, Tiffany, Matthew, Cooper, and Adam. Tell us about them."*

Buck: *"Tiffany is going back to school to be a paralegal; she's not in the business. Matthew is a stuntman and Cooper is deciding on whether he wants to be an actor or not. He lives in Montana and loves to hunt and fish. He doesn't like Hollywood, but he was in* The Postman, *with Kevin Costner. Costner loves him. Cooper can call him up, and Costner will take the call, and they'll just talk. He's a great kid."*

CL: *"Tell us about Adam."*

Buck: *"Adam was my oldest boy. He wanted to be in the movies, he liked to write. His first work was in the TV series* Starman, *with Robert Hays. He appeared in an episode with his grandfather and* me. Then he decided he wanted to be in the production end. He did the work of four or five men, a real good worker.

On Tombstone, he had risen to non-union first assistant director. That's like a master sergeant. He gave this great speech in the beginning of his starting this movie, and I was really amazed. I thought, 'Gee, this is my kid!' Here he is with Kurt Russell and Val Kilmer, he was literally second in command. (Russell and Kilmer stories continue as to them taking control of the direction of the film).

To make a long story kinda short...the guy who wrote Tombstone, Kevin Jarre, was directing and was non-union so they had to hire a non-union assistant, that's when Adam was hired.

The director was fired and the new director who came in was George Cosmatos, a full-blown director, which means that Adam would be the next to go; but he took a liking to Adam and told him he was going to put him in the guild.

Cosmatos told Adam: 'I want you to be my first assistant until I bring in this guy from Europe, and then you're going over into the second unit,' So Adam was in the guild at 25.

So, this great European first assistant director came over from England and George Cosmatos was such a tough director that the great Englishman lasted two weeks. They found him drunk and they had to fire him and bring Adam back because he knew the show, and Adam finished the movie. It wasn't easy because everyone wanted to quit, the producer was so difficult. Bill Fraker the cinematographer wanted to quit and Adam had to make Kurt and Val happy.

You know this is off the subject a little but my dad had this laugh that was more like a cackle, that he was known for. Anyway, nobody could imitate it but Adam. After Maverick (the movie with Mel Gibson, Jodie Foster and James Garner) *my father had a stroke and his vocal cords weren't the same. He was supposed to go in and dub some of his dialogue and his laugh for the movie. He could do the voice fine but, because of what the stroke had done to his vocal chords, he couldn't do the trademark laugh. Adam was the only guy who could do it. So, Adam went in and recorded the laugh and my dad did the voice. So, when you see* Maverick, *you'll hear my dad's voice, but it's Adam doing his grandfather's laugh.*

Anyway, Adam borrowed 55 million dollars to make five movies, with this guy from Beverly Hills, he's 26 at that point and he's in Romania.

I went to Montana for Cooper's graduation from high school and Adam surprised us by showing up. It was a great reunion to see him.

After the graduation, I went down to Ben Johnson's Team Roping, in Houston. Cooper went with me and Matt was working on a mini-series in Texas. I tried to get Adam to come with me and he said no, he wanted to stay and see his mom and ride his brother-in-law's Harley-Davidson.

A week later, he got killed on that motorcycle. So, it went from the happiest to the saddest day of my life...from a graduation to a funeral.

I was extremely proud of him and I am to this day. I miss him but he made a mark, that's for sure. He'll never go away."

CL: *"It was probably a feat just to keep Val Kilmer happy."*

Buck: *"You know, Adam was doing a horror movie right after* Tombstone *and he offered Val Kilmer five million dollars to do this film. At that time that was the most money Val had ever been offered and he said, 'Adam, just tell me one thing. Is this movie any good?' And Adam said, 'No, but we're going to pay you five million dollars.' Val didn't do it. He called me after it happened and he said, 'Adam was really something.'*

I don't know why things happen, but they do and it changes you from time to time; you get bitter but I dove into my work and painted a lot.

And then my dad passed away right after that. Everything just started giving out and I think Adam's passing affected him as well."

The tide would soon turn for Buck however, and a happier chapter in his life began.

Buck: *"I'll tell you a neat story that happened to me. About a year later I was at the World Quarter Horse Show in Texas, and Matthew was with me.*

I had my art gallery set up and Matt was talking to this real pretty girl who had met Adam the year before; Adam was a real big flirt and had flirted with her. I'm listening to this conversation, and she turns and looks at Matt and says, 'You know, you sound just like your brother.' And I said, 'Yep, the legend lives on.'

Well, as I said, this lady in front of me who was looking at something else whirls around and walks over to me and I go, 'Wow! This gal is beautiful!' If I ever had a fantasy woman this was visually how she'd look.

She said, 'I read about you in a magazine.' And I said, 'Please, look at my work.' She did and I knew I had to think fast. I had this guest book and I asked her if she would sign it and she did. Then I asked her if she was married and she said 'no.' And I said, 'Well would you put your phone number down I'd like to ask you out to dinner.' She said, 'I live in New Orleans' and I told her that I didn't care where she lived, so we went out that evening.

She was there at the barrel racing, she's a world class barrel racer. At the end of dinner, I told her I couldn't take my eyes off of her. I told her that when she whirled around and walked over to me she knocked me out. And she said, 'Well, you said the name of my horse,' and I said, 'I did? What did I say?'

And she says to me, 'You said, 'the legend lives on.' I said, 'What's the name of your horse,

Legend?' And she said, 'No, it's The Legend Lives On.'

So, I go back to Matt that night and I said, 'Matt, do you think Adam sent this gal to me?' And he said, 'Definitely,' and I actually believe he did.

The girl Buck is talking about is his beautiful wife, Goldie. As of this writing they have been happily married two years. But there's more evidence to show that she was sent to Buck.

Buck: *"We were in an aisle at the supermarket, this was after we were married, which didn't take long, about 3 months, and she's a southerner and she says, 'Yaw'll want any sausage?' And I said, 'Jimmy Dean Hot?' 'cause that was my dad's favorite, and she said, 'Of course!'*

Then I looked up and said to my dad, 'Now you're involved in it, huh?'

I think that Adam and my dad got together and said, 'Listen, you've cried enough. We're gonna send you something that's going to make you real happy.' And they did.

Goldie makes me laugh and that's important, ya gotta laugh.

My mom taught me a long time ago that 'where you think...you travel. You are the product of your thoughts.' I wouldn't be where I am right now if I hadn't have thought it at one point."

Buck has had sadness in his life, but now things are going his way. His artwork has opened a lot of doors for him career-wise, his film career is stronger than ever, and, of course, there's Goldie. Keep thinking those good thoughts, Buck.

Goldie and Buck Taylor

Addendum 2017: Buck and Goldie have been thinking those good thoughts now for 22 years and no one deserves them more than these two... *The Legends do indeed Live On.*

CHAPTER 8
Johnny Western

*From "Grand Ole 'Autry'" to
"Will Play for 'Cash'" to
"A Real 'Boone' to Johnny's Career"*

It was Johnny Western that gave me the idea for this book at the 1998 Festival of the West during one of the celebrity panels; I brought up the subject of his replacing Johnny Bond with Gene Autry. The conversation went like this:

CL: *"Johnny, who discovered you?"*

Johnny: *"Well, he was a brand-new guy that was trying to get started by the name of Gene Autry* (laughs). *I sure needed a job and Mr. Autry put me under contract when I was just turning 21."*

CL: *"On the 4th of July."*

Johnny: *"Exactly!"*

CL: *"July 1956."*

Johnny: *"Charlie, you oughta write a book and if you do I have an idea I'm gonna be in it, so please write the book!"*

Well, Johnny here you are. I hope I do you justice!

Born in Northfield, Minnesota, Johnny Westerlund aka Western, became interested in western music as a child after seeing his future employer on the silver screen in *Guns and Guitars* (1936).

Vintage Johnny Western

In his early teens, Johnny made his professional debut as the youngest deejay in the country and a singer of country songs on a Northfield radio station. He would go on to perform on local television and began appearing at rodeos on the same bill as the Sons of the Pioneers; it was a singing engagement in 1956 that would change Johnny's life, and catapult him into the big league.

Johnny Bond

Johnny: *"Johnny Bond had left the Gene Autry show after 17 years and Gene was looking for someone to replace him.*

Johnny Bond may not be a well-known name to many western film goers, but he has appeared in over two dozen movies with the likes of Roy Rogers, William Boyd, Don Barry, Johnny Mack Brown, Tex Ritter, Charles Starrett, Jimmy Wakely and Gene Autry."

The Jimmy Wakely Trio was Bond's's introduction into recording and in 1941 he began a 16-year association with Columbia Records. In 1952, he joined the TV show, *Town Hall Party*, as a host, performer, and writer.

A prolific songwriter, Bond would write some of the music industries classic songs such as *Cimarron*, *I Wonder Where You Are Tonight*, *Your Old Love Letter*, and *Tomorrow Never Comes*, forming Vidor Publications in 1955 with friend Tex Ritter.

In 1960, he recorded his popular version of Charlie Ryan's hit song, *Hot Rod Lincoln* for the Republic label with a sequel *X-15* released in 1960; the sequel takes place in the future year of 1997. The Republic Label was not owned by the film studio, Republic Pictures, which ceased production in 1959 to become solely a distribution company.

After leaving Gene in 1956, Johnny Bond returned for the TV version of *Melody Ranch in 1964*, which was televised on Autry's own KTLA in Los Angeles.

When the program ended in 1970, he turned his focus to writing books; in 1976, he wrote a biography on Tex Ritter as well as his own memoirs. In 1978, he also found time to write a book on the recordings of Jimmie Rogers. Johnny Bond passed away that same year, June 12, 1978.

Bond's departure back in 1956 left the door open for a young Johnny Western.

Dick Jones

Johnny: *"Dickie Jones, who was doing* The Range Rider *with Jock Mahoney at the time, called me up and said the Hollywood Christian Group was going to have a Monday night gathering out at a ranch on the edge of town, and he asked if I would come out and sing for the folks? Well, he didn't tell me that the folks were Gene Autry, Roy Rogers, Dale Evans, The Sons of the Pioneers and Susan Hayward among others; and Gene heard me singing at the party.*

I had known Gene for a long time, but he hadn't seen me perform, and two weeks later Johnny (Bond) announced that he wanted to get off the road after seventeen years. Gene Autry called Dickie Jones and said, 'Can you find that Western kid? I need to find someone to replace Johnny Bond.'

So, we signed a contract, actually in June, I went down with Ben Johnson to Oklahoma for the Ben Johnson Memorial Steer Roping, which he did in honor of his father, and that still takes place at the end of June. Ben thought I should play for a lot of people before I go on the Gene Autry show, because we were gonna play for 10 or 20 thousand people on Gene's show.

He piled me in his car and took me to Oklahoma and I played for 12,000 on a Saturday. That was the end of June and then starting on the Fourth of July, at Pueblo, Colorado, I did sell out performances for Gene; so, I got my feet wet really good.

People talk about Elvis Presley or Garth Brooks being hot, and they were and are, but we went from Pueblo to the Canadian National Exhibition, in Toronto, for fourteen days playing two shows a day to three million people; that's how hot Gene Autry was!

Without Gene I couldn't get an agent, but when Gene retired the next year, he put me up with his agent, who got me my first picture. Once you get started in one it kind of snowballs if they like you. I owe everything to Gene."

CL: *"And after those two years with Gene you signed up with Johnny Cash."*

Johnny: *"Cash came out to the west coast to be an actor in* Wagon Train *and he ended up buying Johnny Carson's house when Carson and Ed McMahon went to the east coast to do television.*

He did the part on Wagon Train *(The C. L. Harding Story 1959 with Claire Trevor) and then he put together a package show. Starting on November 1, 1958, we were supposed to play three dates and until Johnny got Parkinson's disease, here about six months ago, we were at 39 years on the road together."* (Johnny Cash passed away on September 12, 2003 due to diabetes complications, less than four months after his wife, June Carter Cash).

In 1957, western music history was made when Johnny Western wrote and sang the theme song, *The Ballad of Paladin*, for Richard Boone's hit western TV series, *Have Gun Will Travel*. The song later became a hit for Cash in the early sixties.

Johnny: "The Ballad of Paladin *didn't start out as the theme for* Have Gun Will Travel. *Most people think that theme song was always a part of the show, but they had some other instrumental music at first.*
I didn't write it as a theme song and I didn't intend to sing it. What happened was, I had appeared on the show and Richard Boone was so helpful and nice to me, that I simply wrote the song as a musical thank you to him."

Richard Boone and Johnny remained good friends until Boone's death; forming a song writing partnership along with *Have Gun Will Travel* creator Sam Rolfe, and later Boone's widow, Claire.

Richard Boone and Johnny during the historic "Ballad of Paladin" recording session.

Along with hit singles such as *Gunfighter* and *Geronimo Gunfighter*, both in 1962, Johnny would continue a healthy recording collaboration with

Johnny Cash; one of their most interesting being a re-interpretation *Bonanza*'s theme song lyrics, originally written by Ray Evans and Jay Livingston and only sung once on the TV show, and a version of *The Rebel*'s theme song *Johnny Yuma*, original lyrics by Andrew J. Fenady.

The most popular western of all time, without a doubt, is *Gunsmoke* and Johnny had the opportunity to spend some time with Marshal Dillion and the gang, and was even able to help Dennis Weaver add a new dimension to his character Chester.

Johnny: *"I got to make some* Gunsmoke *episodes in the black and white days of the '50s with Dennis Weaver and Jim Arness. Those were the half hour shows. They could knock those out in three or four days and I taught Dennis how to play the guitar.*

Remember when Chester would be sweepin' up around the office and he'd sing, 'Run rabbit run, or the dogs'll git ya. Run rabbit run, ya better git away?' Well, Dennis was a big fan of Woody Guthrie and he asked me to come over and teach him how to play about four chords on the guitar so that when he went out on the state fair circuit he could sing those little songs he would sing on Gunsmoke. That's probably what got me on Gunsmoke."

CL: *"You mentioned Ben Johnson a while ago. Wasn't he influential in your film career?"*

Oscar winner & a true gentleman cowboy, Ben Johnson

Johnny: *"I didn't have the $200 to join the Screen Actors Guild in 1957 when I got my first picture, and Ben paid my $200 and sponsored me because you needed a sponsor to get in the guild. $200 in 1957 would be like $2000 today and Ben Johnson wrote them a check, paid my dues, sponsored me, and then we went up to Kanab, Utah* *and shot a picture called Fort Bowie. When I got paid, I was able to pay him back.*

Johnny Western has acted, performed or written music for numerous films and TV shows. He performed with the Sons of the Pioneers while in his mid-teens. He has recorded under contract to Columbia records, performed with the greats like Autry and Cash, and successfully played Las Vegas.

In 1993, he recorded an album entitled, *Johnny Western and the Sons of the Pioneers and Friends*. Incidentally, those friends included Michael Martin Murphey, Red Stegall, and Rex Allen, Sr. & Jr.; as well as being honored in 1998 by Riders in the Sky with their perfect spoof of his song *The Ballad of Paladin*, entitled *The Ballad of Palindrome*.

His career almost ended with a serious Wyoming automobile accident in 1976 which left Johnny with serious injuries and the majority of his bones broken above the pelvis area; he credits Johnny Cash for paying all his hospital bills so he wouldn't have to worry about anything but getting better

Through it all Johnny maintained a regular radio presence on KFDI in Wichita, Kansas where he was on-air daily since 1986.

Johnny: *"Five days a week, from 8:00 in the morning til noon and then I get to run on the weekends and do this stuff."* (Meaning the festivals) (Johnny retired from radio, Saturday, April 10, 2010).

I count Johnny and his lovely wife, Jo, as good friends...they are both a class act. I no way is this a definitive bio on Johnny or any of the other people in this book. I am just blessed to have been a small part of their lives.

Thanks for the idea for this book, Johnny. I hope I did you justice."

Well Earned Awards for Johnny Western
- **TV Theme Hall of Fame (1993)**
- **Country Music Disc Jockey Hall of Fame (2000)**
- **Old Time Country Music Hall of Fame (2000)**
- **Western Music Association Hall of Fame (2001)**
- **Wichita Professional Broadcasters Hall of Fame (2002)**
- **Kansas Cowboy Hall of Fame (2004)**
- **Kansas Western Swing Hall of Fame (2004)**

The Three Johnny's

Left to Right: Johnny Horton, Johnny Cash & Johnny Wester

Epilogue
The Legends aren't Done Yet!

It's been exactly 20 years since I wrote the original book. During that time, I've learned quite a bit and so it was important to update this book.

Not long ago I was visiting my 91-year-old mother at my old childhood home where she still lives. We were sitting in the informal dining room where we would have dinner while watching westerns on the old tube television; my dad installed a custom lazy susan between the family room and the dining area to swivel back and forth for continual viewing while eating.

    I looked to make sure the old lazy susan was still installed between the two rooms. It was there with a modern TV on it. *"I want that Lazy Susan, so I can hang it on my wall,"* I told my mother. *"When I'm done with it, it's yours,"* she said. She understood that among all my other memorabilia this will be my most prized possession.

Charlie LeSueur
April 20, 2017

Other Books by Charlie LeSueur...

*Riding the Hollywood Trail: Tales of the Silver Screen Cowboys.

*Riding the Hollywood Trail: Blazing the Early Television Trail.

*The Illustrated Book of Myths, Legends & Facts Along the Hollywood Trail

Charlie LeSueur is a film historian and author who has dedicated many years to making sure the legends do live on. He is AZ's Official Western Film Historian as well as a college instructor for Central Arizona College, Encore Fellow for the Spirit of the West; Scottsdale's Museum of the West, a film producer and actor. Most of all he would like to thank all those who make this dream possible...all of you.

Why Did I Rewrite This Book?

I really felt it was important to update, revise and correct areas in the original book. I also noticed that there are 'pirate' companies selling the original 1998 book at exorbitant prices I would never pay, nor should anyone else; many of these are marked 'New' which I doubt. These companies latch on to these copies and slap illegally purchased ISBN numbers on them. As such, I felt it was important to update the original.

Made in the USA
Columbia, SC
15 February 2018